Spirits of the Stair

Peter Robinson was born in Salford, Lancashire, in 1953 and grew up mainly in Liverpool. He holds degrees from the universities of York and Cambridge. After teaching for eighteen years at universities in Japan, he is now professor of English and American literature at the University of Reading. The recipient of awards for his poetry and translations, he has also published four volumes of literary criticism, one of prose, and a collection of interviews.

D1581835

KA 0317406 9

By the Same Author

Poetry
Overdrawn Account
Anaglypta
This Other Life
More About the Weather
Entertaining Fates
Leaf-Viewing
Lost and Found
Via Sauro Variations
About Time Too
Anywhere You Like
Ghost Characters
There are Avenues
The Look of Goodbye

Prose
Untitled Deeds

Translations
The Great Friend and Other Translated Poems
Selected Poetry and Prose of Vittorio Sereni
The Greener Meadow: Selected Poems of Luciano Erba

Interviews
Talk about Poetry: Conversations on the Art

Literary Criticism
In the Circumstances: About Poems and Poets
Poetry, Poets, Readers: Making Things Happen
Twentieth Century Poetry: Selves and Situations
Poetry & Translation: The Art of the Impossible

Editor
With All the Views: Collected Poems of Adrian Stokes
Geoffrey Hill: Essays on his Work
Liverpool Accents: Seven Poets and a City
The Thing About Roy Fisher: Critical Studies
Mairi MacInnes: A Tribute

PETER ROBINSON

SPIRITS OF THE STAIR

Selected Aphorisms

Shearsman Books

Exeter

UNIVERSITY OF WINCHESTER
LIBRARY

First published in the United Kingdom 2009 by
Shearsman Books Ltd
58 Velwell Road
Exeter EX4 4LD

ISBN 978-1-84861-062-0
First Edition

Copyright © Peter Robinson 2009

The right of Peter Robinson to be identified as the author of this work
has been asserted by him in accordance with the Copyrights, Designs and Patents
Act of 1988. All rights reserved.

UNIVERSITY OF WINCHESTER

03174069

for Thomas Fisher Robinson

&

Julie Whitehead Redfern

Spirits of the Stair

'y lo que seria peor, hazerse poeta, que segun dizen, es enfermedad incurable, y pegadiza.'
Miguel Cervantes

1

Don Quixote's housekeeper wants the little poetry books in her master's library burned, because, as she says, being a poet is an incurable illness far worse than his knight errancy. But, given his devotion to love and the righting of wrongs, it's surely too late. Don Quixote has already read them.

2

First I wrote to set things to rights. Then, believing that this couldn't be done without reciprocal acts performed in life, I wrote to set them emblematically to rights. Then, finding that this could only be done if there was someone to appreciate the *raison d'être* of the emblem, I put my trust in the reader's role. Just now, fearing that there are hardly any such readers, I'm left with an undiminished urge to write yet precious little sense of what good it might do. Time, perhaps, to return to first principles.

3

Providence too has its limits. Think how much more you can learn from a bad than from a good experience—provided, that is, you survive it.

4

People who always expect the worst can get a reputation for sagacity without having any real foresight: the odds are in their favour. Yet all of life's important decisions are bets against the odds.

5

Being never wrong might well mean failing ever to be usefully right.

6

Every occasion is a combination of things that have happened, which produce it, and things which have not happened, which, if they had, would have prevented it from happening. I arrive at a station (I bought a ticket and the train didn't crash), step down from the carriage (safely) and am kissed by a girl (she's arrived safely too) who later becomes my wife. By this stage my head is spinning. Now multiply by the number of occasions in a life, and the number of human lives.

7

Yesterday my five-year-old daughter told us about a dream in which she gave birth to her mother. But would that be less or more significant if she'd simply invented it to entertain us?

8

To my parents I owe everything ... even the things they didn't give me.

9

A poet has said that genuinely difficult art is truly democratic, and that tyranny requires simplification. So it does. And this would be a nobly democratic idea—if it weren't a simplification.

10

Trapped in your successes, goaded on by setbacks ... How mistaken it is to lose patience with your critics!

11

Randall Jarrell referred to the lyric poet as someone who stands out in the rain for a lifetime hoping once or twice to be struck by lightning.

But who would risk catching pneumonia in the hope of being burnt to a frazzle? No, a poet is a person with a head full of black clouds trying to make it rain.

12

Goethe's reputation: for 'immoral' read 'immortal'.

13

One of the benefits of growing older is that you come to know the exact map references for the nowheres you inhabit.

14

Your wife or husband, flat-mate, whatever, leaves the house early. Expecting her or him home around lunchtime, you leave a message promising to be back about five to make supper. But the other person stays out for lunch and only returns after half past five, having not read your note, when greeted by smells of cooking. Did you make the promise? Did you keep it? The relation of a poem's promise to its imagined reader is like your behaviour and that note.

15

Still though, if it's the artist who makes the promise by means of an artwork, it's the readers who must be there to keep it. And don't think this is a uniquely literary situation either: consider the bank loans and mortgages that have to be paid off by the descendents of those who negotiated them.

16

Across a train's windows, in the floating down to black, a horizon enlivened by lightning forks, you see staggering flow of currency! The base rate reacts by being changed again. In any successful whispering campaign, there's a grain of truth, they speculate, and usually someone else to blame. It's as if the City's job were merely counting money.

17

Set some people down in the middle of a desert and they'll do nothing but complain about the weather. Others will start drawing you a map.

18

You think it slightly sinister, the way I suddenly vanish from your left, and turn up on your right—being deaf, stone deaf on my right side? I'm just giving you the benefit of my one good ear.

19

Keeping away from other people is hardly the best way to escape yourself.

20

A reason for the present decline in the study of history: 'The trouble with the past is that *I* wasn't in it.'

21

Another reason for the same: if you really want to disorientate someone, make sure that they don't know what direction they're coming from.

22

Put 'I' in a poem and I may make a space for others; leave it out and the whole thing is nothing but me.

23

The Muse: a busy person with other interests who hasn't got time for your work.

24

Prejudice: the energy expended in trying to make what is both the same and different feel merely different.

25

How to construct a prejudice: take an adjective in the singular, put a definite article in front of it, and there you are—the English . . .

26

Transience is here to stay.

27

Why does satire seem so plainly out of season? Because the powerful can't take, or even see, the joke—while the rest of us are gagging on the obvious.

28

Fame: it's inevitably a case of mistaken identity.

29

During the questions after a reading, a poet explained to the audience that the autobiographical 'I' in my poetry was a construct. I naturally and politely agreed with this received idea about the fictiveness of autobiography. Later, my host who had been at the event commented that the opinion was quite wrong and that, if anything, I was dismantling the 'I' for inspection, so as to make it understandable to others and myself. This remark had the unexpectedly cheering effect of making 'me' feel understood in a way I hadn't foreseen.

30

If you've given a talk and during the questions somebody begins by asking 'But aren't you just saying…?' it is, of course, possible that the questioner has seen through your sophistications, but possible too that the audience has been invited to think again—and someone's declining the invitation.

31

A small child's need for attention can be simultaneously irritating, inspiring, and sad—so, too, a writer's.

32

Lonely 'geniuses' who don't have a good word for their contemporaries are making at least two mistakes in the one time: they fail to see that self-esteem in a vacuum is merely vanity, and they overlook what makes their contemporaries belong to the same era as themselves.

33

Drink-inspired writing is usually read by stone cold sober readers. Worse, writers on medication for hyperactivity or depression may be feeling better, but their readers aren't necessarily on the same prescription.

34

Unhappiness endured beyond measure can grow into a habit hard to break.

35

People say beauty is only skin-deep, yet in art the skin is deep.

36

Translations *are* like women (and indeed men)—in best cases their beauty and fidelity are wedded together.

37

Is there anything worse than a poet *manqué*? Yes, a critic *manqué*.

38

Some writers—when you send them 'best regards' and hope that things are 'going well' for them—immediately send you back a list of their latest and forthcoming achievements. Once I thought the only response was to behave differently. Now I think it depends on cases. In the above, I reciprocate with choice excerpts from the *curriculum vitae*. And that's the last I hear from them.

39

While attempting to talk around my then situation, I was once smartly advised: 'Don't run yourself down, there are plenty of people to do that for you.' But what others think of me is really their business. Mine is with seeing the case in perspective.

40

If misery is handed down from generation to generation, then it's no surprise that when I'm angry or depressed you hear the sound of an eighteenth-century farm labourer who finds himself forced to beg for work in a factory slum.

41

However untimely, when it comes death is always on time.

42

Here to stay, though gone tomorrow—that's all a writer hopes of life.

43

How difficult it is to put yourself under an obligation to someone you don't really like!

44

What I can't or couldn't say, and why not—these are some of the things that spur me into poetry. The poems are often placed between a speaker and an indicated or implied listener. It's as if I were talking to you, saying what I couldn't in a real situation—in a form that explains why, and yet preserves, in the poetic occasion, the impossibility of my speaking.

45

When the poems are read by others, and by those involved, the real situations alter again. Thus, as I do it, poetry becomes a part of life, of a life held in common differences. The poems are founded on intimacies because such private relations between people are what speakers of a language variously share.

46

Spending many years in Japan is like going to the toilet in the dead of night without turning the light on: nothing changes, but after a while you don't bump into the furniture quite so often.

47

We are united by what separates us; but the art is in making that appreciated.

48

My fear of death has changed: it used to be the thought of what in life I'd miss which upset me; now it's the fear for what my near ones would lose. So I'm happier when we all fly together. But what about being upset by the things they would miss in life, should we die at the same time? I'm no better: just the character of my self-concern has changed.

49

Beware long afternoon shadows of branches and tree trunks at winter's end.

50

You want to talk about our relationship? Don't forget that our words will change the thing you think we're talking about even as we utter them.

51

A quick and sharp tongue is frequently mistaken for a good brain. Why? Perhaps it's because you're likely to feel the full force of the former, but you'll only be granted small access to the latter.

52

You can usually judge a mind by the quality of its mistakes.

53

In societies where trading in death is a way of life, the news headlines are usually filled with an empty air of shock.

54

Global warming: just how much evidence is there for an increase in warmth between the richer and poorer nations?

55

Faced down by a window filled with blossoms at their best, just pause a while.

56

So your publisher has occasion to describe your sales as 'glacial'— meaning, presumably, that you sell small numbers over periods of silence and slow time. Yet, sadly, what with the climate changes and all, the glaciers are melting.

57

Like falling asleep after making love, when it no longer needs to continue, a sentence should come to a full stop.

58

While not pretending to exhaust its subject, an aphorism should certainly wear itself out.

59

I have lost a friend: as she withdrew from life, I tried to make myself an exception to the rule; but her growing loss of attachment to things made me seem to have them the more, which is why I too had first to be offended then finally driven away.

60

Good translators must be tied to the mast so they can hear, but not be hypnotized by, the siren calls of their own interpretations.

61

So many cherished friends and acquaintances seem like substitutes for my parents and siblings—the sorts of mothers or fathers, brothers and sisters I imagine I'd have liked to have, but didn't. Yet it's hardly surprising, given this compulsion to recruit others into the family romance, that they should sooner or later fail to match my over-weaning need even more than the ones I have to get along with, the ones there wasn't the chance to choose in the first place.

62

Less cant, more candour . . . that would make a change.

63

On a poetry critic writing a review: it's as if you had held up a mirror to Dame Nature herself and then found exactly reflected there the landscape of her own mind.

64

When it comes to readers, it seems I prefer the particular to the general.

65

It's all very well to pretend to save the victims of realism by attempting to make them think that the world is how they imagine it to be, and can therefore be changed with a thought experiment, but where does this leave the victims of reality?

66

The point of no return is precisely the place from which you will have to find a way home.

67

Good poems are disarming.

68

Suppose a solipsistic state were possible in which everything was 'mine'. In it I would have no need to use the word because nothing would be anything else anyway. That I do use the word 'mine' to identify certain ideas, things, and feelings rather rules solipsism out as an irrelevance. The fact that some ideas, things, and feelings are identifiable as 'mine' implies that there are also other people's contrastively present in what some would like to call 'my' world—and, I have no reason to doubt, vice-versa.

69

Reviewers accuse poets of 'solipsism' because whatever emotive charge the poems under review have can be denied and temporarily neutralized by insinuating that they fail to be emotions about and for other people.

70

A gap in curtains lets through one more slice of night—and why ever not?

71

How curious that there should be so little mutual warmth and respect between readers, writers, and critics—since a large number of those involved fulfil all three roles, and a composing poet will be fulfilling them all at the very same time!

72

The only way for an artist to describe a cultural situation is imaginatively from inside it.

73

In best cases, poems claim less and deliver more: their descriptions are by definition limited in scope, are a seeing from the inside, and are impacted with experience, emotion, and idea. If poems arrive late and confused on the scene, they have, again in best cases, more staying power because they are more thoroughly embedded in the culture and occasion to which they belong.

UNIVERSITY OF WINCHESTER LIBRARY

74

In poetry the best way to fly is to be well grounded.

75

So how, as poets grow older, do they manage not to rest on their lack of laurels?

76

Beware those poets whose only recorded admirations are for writers long ago and far away—writers, that is, who offer no immediate threat to the admirer's self-esteem, and who are equally helpless to resist being conscripted into these shows of solidarity with the distant great.

77

Poetry, thou art translated! (Even an ass of a rendering can prove the object of a reader's love and devotion).

78

What's produced by the overthrow of an illusion need not be a truth, merely a counter-illusion—e.g. the death of God.

79

Just as a half-rebuilt house is probably uninhabitable, so too is a renovated cliché.

80

The implied reader is someone particularly suited to understand these words.

81

My ideal reader has chosen to spend time with these words in particular.

82

An aphorism is a well-used dishcloth waiting to be wrung out.

83

Metaphors are icebergs: you're dazzled by the similarity visible on the waves; but get too close and you'll be sunk by the vast unlikeness beneath the surface.

84

On more than one occasion, at a party or reading, the most critically decisive moment about a poet's work has been when he—and it always has been a he so far—threatens me with physical violence.

85

Try to live by the pen, and you'll die by the pen.

86

I read that in Britain now there's an undeclared war going on between the Academy and Grub Street about who shall be the arbiter of literary value—but as distinct constituencies neither has seemed particularly inclined to give poetry its due.

87

You're exasperated by academic critics, freelance reviewers, prize-giving committees, chat-show hosts, back-scratching in-crowds, jobs-for-the-boys clubs? What matters in the longer run is whether you have a modicum of dedicated and devoted readers, some of whom may well be writers themselves, who pass a taste for your things on to the coming generations. But the problem is that the characters above may or may not actively hinder your finding those readers.

88

What's it to be, Academia or Grub Street? Well, look at all the writers who've found it more rewarding (in a number of senses) to succumb to the deserved patronage of the former than to perish from neglect in the latter.

89

Even if the best poetry manages to be simultaneously made to measure and *prêt-à-porter*, your high street shopper still won't wear it.

90

Good poems resolve emotions; bad ones provoke them.

91

Far more ink has been spilt by philosophers discussing the question of whether Crusoe could have invented a private language than he himself had on his island when drawing up a contract with the Spaniards.

92

Though Robinson may or may not have been capable of inventing a private language, why, since he could already speak English, some Portuguese, Spanish, and perhaps other languages too, would he have ever felt the need to do so?

93

Philosophical examples seem so often at a tangent to poetic metaphors. Like icebergs with nothing below the surface, they may dazzle and be harmless, but they don't stay afloat for very long.

94

Forgetting is given us for survival (I read), but the best way to forget something for good is first to remember it properly.

95

A writer without a developed critical faculty is like a car without adequate brakes—ruinous for all concerned.

96

Sad, angry, or embittered clowns: a sense of humour is by no means the same as a sense of comedy.

97

At least married people who are not native speakers of the same language may be less likely to assume that they can read each other like books.

98

Being a fifth columnist in the fourth estate is not going to win you many friends among your contemporaries.

99

'Speaking as a poet . . .': that's how a person who had published some verse would preface each of his interventions at a literary society's committee meetings. Behaving so ineptly as regards his presumed vocation and status didn't, of course, rule out his being a poet, but it strongly hinted that he couldn't be a good one.

100

You think there's a life of the mind? Catch a cold and think again.

101

The inability to wish somebody well must be a form of self-betrayal.

102

It has crossed my mind that I'm writing these observations to protect the poems I might yet write from the temptation to versify ideas already formed, or half-formed, in the back of my head. But it shouldn't surprise me to find I've been all this time turning into an epigrammatic poet.

103

The right place for artists is the dunce's corner they've painted themselves in, from where, despite the temptation to pussy-foot back across the still wet paint of recent work, the only way out is to imagine a new room behind your back and, without looking round, step smartly into it.

104

A novelist remarks that creative writers have no special insight that could justify their getting involved in political controversy. They are like everyone else. Precisely: that's why they have every right to become involved.

105

According to the doctrine of Original Sin, humanity is a tainted brand.

106

People who cannot take pleasure in others' successes are unlikely to enjoy many of their own.

107

One problem with thinking that your race or nation is God's chosen people, or has God on its side, is that you have built your tribal self-esteem on an illusion. Another is that for there to be equality among peoples you will first have to feel robbed of your birthright.

108

The habits of the addict and the reader are evidently different in kind. Who ever heard of street crimes being committed to fuel a craving for poetry books?

109

Talk about silence!

110

Two temptations: the first, to show the self-contradictoriness of statements that betray their idea in the language of their utterance; the second, to show how statements are suffering from bewitchments of language, their buried structures or embedded assumptions demonstrably preventing clarity of idea. But couldn't those attacked on either ground always appeal to the other temptation by way of a defense or mitigation? And isn't there the further dilemma of when best to succumb to the one temptation and when to the other?

111

For a poet, all reading is close reading—which may explain why some of them have such difficulty getting through novels.

112

One way to avoid ending up like your parents is consciously to imitate them.

113

Doing book reviews can so often feel like being one of those lovers talking in bed: how difficult it is to find words 'not untrue and not unkind'.

114

The effort of finding some benefit in a poet's work can be excruciating.

115

People often behave as if they were a *terra incognita* to themselves, and especially when they claim self-understanding.

116

Understanding ourselves is like reaching an itch in the small of the back—more easily done with the help of someone else.

117

Ruthlessly honest as you may have to be about your own work, still you must also be generosity itself when it comes to what other people write.

118

An acquaintance that took her own life has communicated more to me since she died than during the time we were acquainted. When she was alive and married I'd all but forgotten her. Now I can't get her out of my mind.

119

Having less time for the peripheral as we grow older could well be the result of the dual awareness that there is so much less time left to do the most important, and that the resources of energy with which to do them are so depleted. It needn't indicate any reduction in the zest for life, just a lessening in the capacity to appreciate it. And so the frustrations of youth give way to those of old age.

120

Is it possible that poets write less as they get older because they feel too *au fait* with life? As the areas of uncertainty and puzzlement are reduced by habituation and repeated recognition, there seems that much less to make sense of through finding a meaningful form? Then poets who write into old age must either have learned how to feed their uncertainty, or how to write a more knowing kind of poem? Would that be the explanation?

121

As regards the pretensions, even the pretentiousness, of younger writers—be tolerant. They need their self-belief to keep going, and may well have precious little upon which to build it.

122

Equally, it will happen that 'pretentious' is merely the word used by those with power to brand those who would claim a little space to do something ambitiously different.

123

Perhaps you can't hope to amend your life by revising a cadence, but there are far worse things to do with your time.

124

Readers are treated with the utmost respect when left to look after themselves.

125

A 'legendary' poet and scholar (as he's described on a press release) once criticized a book of mine for its lack of jokes—yet, now I come to think of it, I can't recall a single witticism in his entire oeuvre. But, be fair, perhaps he was advising me to learn from his mistakes.

126

I am *required* to tell more jokes. How's that for a start?

127

No amount of art will compensate for a ruined life, but who's to say the life would not have been ruined anyway?

128

Coming across your own books in a shop can't fail to cut both ways. They've been distributed. Yes, but they've not been bought.

129

'You'll be buried in Westminster Abbey,' said my first wife at a dinner party once, 'in the tomb of the unknown poet.'

130

I'm to be buried in the tomb of the unknown poet? Ah well. At least it won't be lonely.

131

Another of my first wife's witticisms about the life of the struggling poet: 'You're the only man I know who gets rejected at least five times before breakfast.'

132

Submitting to magazines *is* like punching yourself in the face. After a while, at least you don't recognize who's doing the punching. So it's that bit more difficult to feel the shame.

133

If 'travel', 'travail', and 'trouble' aren't etymologically related, then they certainly should be! Whatever . . . they're a torture.

134

Like seeing the world through a mosquito net, the artist creates an overall harmony by making innumerable minute distinctions.

135

More than one reviewer has expressed a discomfort at poems of mine that are dedicated to named interlocutors. They sense themselves marginal to the communicative occasion, and feel like they're hearing half a conversation through a wall. They mistake the poetic evocation of an expressive moment's intimate candour for a private exchange, or they think there's more to be explained when, in fact, the poem's shape has already had the last word.

136

That a named interlocutor is also a poetic convenience has not been lost on one or two of my dedicatees. They have resented the words they appear to occasion.

137

A young poet once told me he wouldn't read the very distinctive work of a senior writer because he didn't want to be influenced. He was, you understand, in the process of constructing a narrowly distinctive manner of his own.

138

But a poet with a natural gift can imitate everything and anyone. The outcome will always be a surprise.

139

Consolation, like beauty, is a by-product of art. Readers can be left to find it according to need. Poets won't produce it by trying to put it into their work, and they'd be fools to try.

140

Good writers on poetry keep their experience of reading and their understanding of the things read in a continuous dialogue with each other.

141

Subjectivity in art is a communal adhesive.

142

The prison-house of language? A living language is not only the innumerable things that everyone who speaks it can say, or they and their forebears have said, but also all that they and their descendents will say, or even might have said, for that matter.

143

Only frequent the works of your era's greatest sensibilities, writes a neglected poet and editor. To take his advice would have meant not receiving it.

144

The contemporary poet in residence is expected to wear the cap and bells without either the benefit of access to power or the freedom to bite the hand that feeds.

145

Talk about 'the patron and the jail'! I do hope the poet in residence with a local police force will at least take the opportunity to put two author photos on the back of his next book—one from the front and one the side.

146

There are intelligences whose aim seems to be to see through everything. Spend some time with them and there's nothing like bumping into people and things.

147

How noble the poet who gave up a writing fellowship when he couldn't write on it—yet how inartistic of him to take its terms so literally!

148

Learning not to care what people say or write about your work is like living a premature posthumous existence.

149

Goethe writes that poetry can accompany you through life, but it can't be a guide. Yet there are travelling companions whose recommendations at crossroads are well worth a listen.

150

Trying to write a convincing poem about an event in life is the best way of finding out what you really felt about it. Being unable to write one is a sure sign of something—but what that something might be will require you to think out for yourself.

151

In *Hamlet*, Shakespeare writes a tragedy about the reluctance to take revenge. In his *Inferno*, Dante takes horrific revenge while pretending to be shocked and disturbed by what has become of his so-called friends or enemies—and, now and then, what might become of him too.

152

When Catholic believers approach death, which do they fear more—the pains of Purgatory, or the shadow of a possibility that after their decease there will be just nothingness?

153

Proposed emendation for *Hamlet*, act 2, scene 2, lines 251–2: 'there is nothing either good or bad *and* thinking makes it so.'

154

Eroticism and tenderness make strange bedfellows.

155

Death, after all, is not the end of the world.

156

My dad tells how once he was walking with members of his regiment beside a railway embankment somewhere in Italy during the war when an American troop train went by. The carriage windows were all thrown open and those strolling British soldiers from the Intelligence Corps were showered with chocolate, tinned rations, boots, bits of uniform, and other foreshadowings of the Marshall Plan. The GIs must have thought them local peasants. It was much the same with volumes of contemporary American poetry in my youth.

157

'And she doesn't understand my jokes,' an Englishman married to a Japanese woman once complained. 'I didn't know you'd ever made one,' was the only reply that came to mind.

158

A poet writes of England that our island story is over—which sounds like an idea on the very cutting edge of this not so brave new world. But what if the story isn't over, merely at the beginning of a freshly unpredictable chapter? Thus the modish starts to sound démodé, even in its hey-day.

159

The island stories, of Britain and Japan for instance, seem like tireless attempts to persuade their struggling and often migrating populations that transit lounges are arrival gates.

160

It's considered all right for an Irish, Welsh, Scottish, and many another poet to be a nationalist—but not, heaven forbid, for an English writer.

And there's a good reason for this: embracing nationalism may always be a mistake, but for the English poet it would be a *serious* one.

161

'The eternal' and 'immortality' are also among art's side effects. Aim for them, and you're sure to miss.

162

The career and reception of some post-war English poets reveal the difficulties in being even a patriotic writer in a de-colonizing and post-imperial epoch. Their patriotism (one tested, it should always be remembered, by the boredoms and horrors of world conflict) could so easily be mistaken for, or haplessly slide into, a reactive nationalism. Yet, still, there are intimately fraught feelings of attachment to, and repulsion from, the places where we first drew breath which make even such patriotism seem a bit of driftwood to which, indeed, a scoundrel might conveniently cling.

163

I'm getting old: my jacket has some slight foxing—and so, come to think of it, does my skin.

164

Generational change is likely to be mistaken for a series of losses. That's because the more powerful elders doing the lamenting aren't usually in the best position to appreciate any of the compensatory gains.

165

'You must come to dinner some time,' he said. But I knew from his grammar that we'd never meet again.

166

People may well accuse me of being merely a domestic interior and love poet, but I would have to ask them if they think that the contemporary public and political world will some day rise to having poems written about it.

167

The worst of lovers' quarrels—in my experience—have tended to be about bank accounts and houses.

168

Why do literary people who should know better keep insisting that the aesthetic and the cultural are in non-communicating, hermetically sealed chambers? They don't appear to realize they're denigrating and dehumanizing both.

169

One difficulty with success is that it usually comes, if it comes, when you've long ago had to grow out of the need, or even desire, for any success at all.

170

The best way to avoid losing people and things is to let them go.

171

My shelf of autographed copies: a mortuary filled with lost friends.

172

How extraordinary it is to find myself being reminded by the reviewer of a new would-be epic that prejudicial, opinioned doggerel is not poetry! Sometimes it seems as if everything has been opportunistically forgotten by the in a hurry and the on the make.

173

Are imaginative people doomed to find their environments ever so slightly under-stimulating?

174

The independently wealthy seem so pointless to themselves.

175

In England even my family and friends used to say that I didn't know how to handle money—but no one was offering me much practice at doing it.

176

For decades my father has suffered from persecutory nightmares. Is it possible I've inherited his dream life?

177

Face your demons on a nightly basis, but don't get too familiar with them.

178

For other people: take off the boxing gloves, put on the kid ones.

179

Do unto yourself as you would do unto others.

180

Though they so frequently include landmarks and historical events, reviewers keep insisting that my poems create a time and place of my own imagining. This is a side of their reception, such as it is, which I find harder and harder to explain. Is it because the poems fail to jolly those readers along with a steady supply of common understandings, reference points, and received ideas? The alternatives (whether limits or limitations in my work or the reviewers') are even more disturbing to suppose.

181

Why was I at all upset by hearing about the death of a university contemporary whom I hadn't heard from in a quarter of a century? Hadn't he been a long time dead for me already?

182

Intrinsic value? Just one more pre-emptive strike on the future doomed to miss its target.

183

From a tangle of travels and journeys, I find myself returning to my old alma mater to attend a guest lecture of some kind. The place is so much more overgrown than it was—with trees and chalet-like houses amongst them. When I'm inside the building where the lecture's to be held, it turns out to be the foyer of an enormous teaching hospital, the refreshment zone for a shopping mall. But the corridors are more like an art museum, even to the prints of old houses in Japan. I approach the receptionist and ask for some guidance, but now she's an arts administration officer and proceeds to write me a handful of cheques. I protest that it wouldn't be right to take them. I don't have anything to spend them on; but she insists, telling me to go and buy a car. At which point I realize … and another day begins.

184

When I suffered my meningitis-like relapse after the brain tumour removal and was back in hospital on intravenous medication for a couple of weeks, I found myself behaving like a lapsed atheist.

185

So why is it that I'm able to bank my failures and live off their capital, but I can't do the same with my successes? This impaired capacity to enjoy achievements can hardly be construed as a virtue.

186

There's an evident falsity—one damaging to relations with younger, older, and more struggling writers—in having achieved things but failing at the same time to foster any sense of inner achievement.

187

The compulsion to keep working in middle age may well be fuelled by the tendency for late-coming achievements quickly to seem delusory, or to be written off because gained by the worthless little creature who had to keep doggedly on through years of disappointment and set-back.

188

Carnivalesque nationalism in football crowds, and such like, wouldn't be such an eerie thing if the farcical parody didn't so consort with its tragic precursor.

189

How do I define my nationality? No need, others are only too willing to do that for me.

190

The bad magic of modern fame is nowhere more evident than in the shrines set up to much loved, financially successful, musicians—a Verdi, or a Paul McCartney, for instance. The absence of aura in their birthplaces is so at odds with the pilgrimage industry's marketing of non-events to simple souls.

191

How difficult it is to work without hope, simply for the pleasure of doing it. You'd think that working were itself a form of hoping for the best.

192

However much individual poets cherish the differences between their work and that of contemporaries, in a very few years they will all be seen to have produced the characteristic texts of that period.

193

The sabre-rattling leader of a country, thinking he was commenting on the unacceptable behaviour of his enemy, once described the present situation as 'like the re-run of a bad movie'. It shows an unenviable economy with words to have condemned himself out of his own mouth, and haplessly to have echoed Karl Marx's observation about history, tragedy, and farce all in the same breath.

194

Self-denial: neither treating yourself, nor treating your self.

195

Today I was just starting to give a lecture about 'On Myself' by Anne Finch, Countess of Winchelsea, when, looking up from the text, I noticed a student's plastic bag with the words AN OBJECTIONABLE GIFT printed on it. The mere sight started a crowd of thoughts on the place of poetry in life, and I said nothing at all for what seemed like two or three minutes.

196

Socio-biological reductionism in action: an academic once wanted to convince me that poetry was a survival from the species' primitive courting rituals. It was, of course, one now outdated and therefore pointless, empty, defunct. Thus he managed simultaneously to demonstrate a breathtaking capacity neither to understand the meanings and uses of cultural products, nor to appreciate their value, nor, indeed, to show any sensitivity towards another person's evident *raison d'être*. And he also said he didn't like my poems!

197

But don't forget that bullies come in all shapes and sizes.

198

Behind the glass of the Travel Shop window I couldn't hear a word they were saying; but the young couple's stance and gestures betrayed what had come between them. Then just as suddenly they were gone, the manager after them, out of sight—the abandoned customers looking around with smiles between amusement and concern. Come back, by way of apology and for our sakes, the travel agent simply said, 'I thought he was going to clock her one.'

199

However much they may appreciate, works of art in bank vaults—or gallery deposits, for that matter—are non-performing assets.

200

'Whose creature are you?' asked a distinguished professor of literature as we sat down to lunch. 'And how is it you live?' Though in my mid-twenties, I was so naive about how this world worked that the first question made no sense, and, when he explained, I could only reply that I was no one's. To the latter, I said I was making ends meet with bits of part-time teaching. Now, I realize, his questions were not of that kind at all. To the first I should have replied: 'Pray tell me, sir, whose dog are you?' And to the latter: 'Employment hazardous and wearisome!' But, on second thoughts, no, my clay-footed half-comprehension was by far the better way to get out of there alive.

201

In England once, being driven towards some traffic lights, I heard the driver mutter with reference to some windscreen cleaners waiting to ply for trade, 'We've got to get these people off the streets.' My finding the comment despicable was only equaled by a resentment at the assumption that I would share his feeling that here, rather than a bit of plucky capitalistic enterprise, was a social nuisance waiting to be tidied away.

202

I regret I'm not able to keep up meaningful relationships with all the friends I've ever had—but I fear they don't harbour anything like the same feeling about having known me!

203

The one problem in meeting up with old friends after many years is that it may just serve to underline why you lost touch with each other in the first place.

204

Through the years of living abroad as an economic emigré, a self-perpetuated exile, expatriate, or what you will, I have never worried about the need to preserve my Englishness. *That* is something I'll never escape.

205

My characteristics as an Englishman are things that those around me, whether in Japan or Italy, make much more of than I could ever do.

206

To the English language I owe not only my identity and vocation, but also my living. Now how could I ever repay all that?

207

Poets (and the rest of us) are forever having to find new ways for turning our germs into gems.

UNIVERSITY OF WINCHESTER
LIBRARY

208

The very thing that prompts you to start a piece of writing may be just what you'll have to leave behind to finish it.

209

Two types of poetic occasion: emotion recollected while you're feeling it; emotion that comes back to you months later with significance you weren't aware of at the time. In each case, you'll have had to wait for the lived prompting to evolve as a form of words and phrases with direction and implication. Yet in the first case it's better to try and forget you've promised yourself that 'there's a poem here', while in the second you can be thankful that something was germinating without you even being aware of it.

210

Writers might aim both to show and invite understanding.

211

The life of a language depends on its being able to contain conflict: it must be able to bear difference within its usages; it must be able to mediate and mitigate confrontation. Without the former it would have no dynamic growth, without the latter no possibility of forming the medium for any cultural cohesion.

212

Just as we have social workers that must measure their responses according to the problems being addressed, so too we have social writers whose work is adjusted to assumptions about their readers' and audiences' needs and incapacities. Yet art is not damage-specific, as pharmaceutical products usually are. It cannot be engineered to fit the target disease, and just to the extent that writers attempt to make it do so, so will it be unfitted for its true—and in large measure—unpredictable purposes.

213

Poets have to find their own new ways of making sense of the world, but their methods must grow and change within communities and the languages that they speak. The danger of living and working in your own culture is that you don't find new ways; you parrot the senses felt to be demanded by your community and time. The problem with living in isolation is that your new ways have only attenuated relations to your community's self-understandings. I could say that you might as well take your pick of predicaments, but the fact is you usually just don't have much choice.

214

The meanings of art and life come not from mysterious depths, but out of profound surfaces.

215

If 'Le style est l'homme même', then to have a number of styles would mean to be a handful of different people?

216

A problem with reading the works of Fernando Pessoa's heteronymic characters is that, however much furnished with the trappings of biography, none of them ever quite rises to providing the literary experience of a wholly complex person. But the worst of it is that, as a result, neither does their author, even when he writes as Pessoa.

217

Poetry is an exploration of possibility. It's not usually a search for identity, but a searching of identity. Most of us have too much going on inside us that the social world has no use for. Poetry can be a means for resisting the unnatural wastage in having a life too insistently adapted to those uses.

218

Becoming a person requires many recognitions of what I am not and cannot be; but the person I thus become can be depleted and undernourished if it doesn't have space to move and change, to identify itself with what it is not, to approach in imagination the experience of others. We can be both over- and under-defined for all manner of personal, cultural and political motives. Poetry is simultaneously engaged in elucidating and loosening the forms of definition we inhabit.

219

Nowadays, we don't need a Plato to banish poets from the city. We have literary critics, and poets too, to keep us squabbling in sectarian ghettos.

220

If religion were the opium of the people, what would that make the soul? I ask merely for information.

221

The reciprocity of art is in its meaning.

222

It was as if all the world's injustices were to be represented by the sound of a football referee's whistle.

223

If supporting a team is always a waste of your own time, why do supporters' tears of grief seem so much hollower than their tears of joy? When your team wins, the attempt to fend off meaninglessness is rewarded with an illusion (you feel your own horizon flush with the chances of success); when your team loses, its failure underlines both your own closed-down vistas of possibility, and your craving for reassuring illusions.

224

When I allow myself to get involved in supporting one side or another in an international football match, no matter what the teams, I can't help sensing a trace of self-betrayal.

225

As a youngish poet I would enthusiastically try to translate verse by authors from languages in which I would not have claimed fluency. Two or three times, I was rebuked for my efforts and humiliated by diplomats (or the wives of diplomats) from the countries in which those authors, when young, were themselves rebuked, humiliated, or worse.

226

When translating the work of poets, it's not enough to understand their native language. You must also have the humility to teach yourself their contribution to that language.

227

Poets with a distinctive manner who write and then publish too much give their work more than an air of planned obsolescence.

228

There are quite a few well-received poets nowadays whose works give the strong impression that they have either never learned, or have unlearned, how to live with and cherish individual poems.

229

One way to try and stop behaving like a child is to become a parent.

230

Watching mothers and fathers relate to their babies you'd think the first aim of the latest generations were to infantilize their progenitors.

231

Reviewers will praise young poets for finding a voice; but if you want to find a voice, you must of course first lose one.

232

A poet's 'voice' in our day is usually a by-product of vocalized writing, rather more than of transcribed speech. So the best thing to do if you want to find a voice is evolve a style—and, while you're at it, why not try for one that will grow and change as you do?

233

Better still: develop a repertoire of possibilities whose outermost limits are not known to anyone, even yourself.

234

A good voice isn't lost as the owner ages. It's just that the original purity of timbre will usually have surrendered itself to the textures of loss.

235

What's the difference between a travelling salesman and a poet giving readings? Precious little. If anything, the salesman has the advantage of being relatively free to change firms and so represent a different product as the market changes. Not so the poet.

236

Many wise people have said that love is an illusion, that we love our idea of the other person and not that person as such. Yet even such an understanding of love, to result in so much as a date, must be strong enough to sponsor the making and keeping of promises. This is how the illusions turn into behaviour, and take on a life of their own.

237

Poets who are obsessed with their quotation on the stock exchange of status and opinion have mistaken their vocation; but poets are people too, and should be forgiven for the occasional lapse of concentration.

238

An embassy issues a statement to the effect that it doesn't want to hear any remarks that call for understanding of its desperate and murderous enemies. While to understand something is not to condone it, this communiqué reveals the suspicion of sympathy assumed to be required for such an act of intelligence. But why does the Embassy not call for understanding of its side's position? A mutual understanding? That's the last thing they want to further their interests.

239

Nothing more hackneyed than the idea that you're an original; it merely means you're too self-deluded to be bothered finding out what and who you've been imitating unawares.

240

The writer who despises reformers—because they are physicians who won't heal themselves before anyone else—overplays his hand when he adds that if you set out to heal yourself first you'll spend a lifetime on the task. If self-reform will take up all of your time anyway, should you wish to complete any work in your life, you'll have to do something else.

241

Sometimes I feel like a little boy trespassing in the Garden of Eden so as to filch an apple from the Tree of Knowledge—but the tree's bare. It's already been taken. Even so, I'm still obliged to accept the blame.

242

It is possible to become so contented with a present situation, and equally realistic about yourself, that you don't even want your dreams to come true.

243

The best poets seem able both to hook a big one and then throw it back alive.

244

Just as there are society painters, so too 'society poets'—hapless creatures who write what they have every right to believe is their own work, but which turns out merely to satisfy the taste of the time and is rightly forgotten when it passes.

245

Nowadays many a politician—and not only Tory novelists—behaves like the bad writer whose sole concern is to maintain a market share by appearing to give the public exactly what his agent tells him it wants.

246

The best way to overcome envy is to achieve things—in your own terms.

247

It's true enough that you skim a newspaper article for what you can get out of it, the gist, but to do the same with a poem will get you less than nothing—why? Because the newspaper reader takes, while the poetry reader has to be involved in give-and-take. It's not quite that 'we receive but what we give', merely that if you don't give of yourself, you won't receive what it has to offer.

248

Yet if you want to read *anything*, even a menu, the best way is to treat it like poetry—for, if it doesn't respond, you'll at least be in a position to order.

249

None of this denies in the least that reading newspapers and reading poetry are activities of the very same kind—merely that they invite and expect different degrees of involvement.

250

A person who tells you they were 'lucky' to get a prestigious post is more likely to be attempting to disarm your presumed resentment than expressing a true recognition of marginal fitness for the position attained. But since you don't feel any such resentment, or inclination to flatter by brushing aside the luck, this appearance of modesty stands out as transparently false.

251

Bernard Williams writes in passing of how with certain activities 'The trick is to combine knowing what I am doing with not thinking about it'. One of these is surely composing poetry, and, perhaps, of making any kind of art. It involves a form of self-overlooking. You feel both intensely focussed on something, and freed—often only briefly—from fret about the outcome. Even making crucial revisions can feel like this, despite the necessary presence of the critical faculty and the archeological strata of 'know-how' and 'better not' being deployed at such a speed as hardly to constitute reflection.

252

At the height of the vogue for Aids-related fiction I gave a reading with one of its principal exponents, who pointedly asked in the questions session whether as a poet I found death a rich vein. But what made him think anyone could have cornered the market in dying?

253

Why is self-scepticism so important in a writer? Because a vast amount of what people call understanding is opinion they require so that they can maintain a precarious equilibrium. The more you can rid yourself of the need to cling to such attitudes, the more you approach the understanding of things. Self-scepticism is not the final state of mind, but the route to that state in which understandings start.

254

Even judges can make Freudian slips: for 'fragrant' read 'flagrant'.

255

Early this morning I dreamed of being back in the north of England again. I was running to catch a train for an evening in London with a young woman (one that resembled nobody I know or have known) who, just as we were about to set off, leaned over and kissed me. Even as this was happening, or very soon after, I knew it was only a dream. Yet what most reinforced the feeling after I awoke was not only the clear memory of that young woman and that kiss, but the fact of my mind's being still able to produce such a dream.

256

You know when your eyesight's really going if you are obliged to keep books at arm's length so as to read them.

257

A professor gives a talk deploring the distractions of the present era. A much younger member of the audience raises a qualm about one small point. The professor then brushes this quickly aside. The proponent of focus and attraction is thus defended from the distractive force in another's point of view. Yet to be so armoured against a qualifying dialogue itself betrays symptoms of chronic distraction.

258

'You're good with words,' said a literary critic; but it didn't sound anything like a compliment.

259

Nothing more fatal to a friendship than a sequence of conversations in which the confidences are all coming from one side only …

260

Being a touchy fellow at the best of times, I used to be irritated beyond measure when my contemporaries, even the ones who had committed themselves on my work, would greet me with a cry of 'Here comes the poet!'

261

Marcel Duchamp made a point of mocking a merely retinal art—although, strictly speaking, there can be no such thing. Now, as if capitalizing on his perhaps joking insight, we have merely mental art.

262

There's nothing like a *rappel à l'ordre* in art to aggravate the chaos.

263

Beware those who have an explanation for everything. So often an explanation is meant to get rid of something, to explain it away. But to understand you first have to accept, to be understanding of something, to give it your understanding.

264

Far too much is premised on the idea that in order to understand you must be a detached observer. So those who *do* can't see, and those who *see* can't do. The evident falsehood of this is one reason why I like art as life and vice-versa—for to see is to do and you usually can't do without seeing. People who enjoy art ought really to be appreciating life better because they are living it with added value. Yet only too often the meaning of one seems to point to the hollowness of the other. Then something is plainly wrong with either, or your attitude to either, or both.

265

It's often said we ought to treat people as ends and not means, but people shouldn't be treated as either ends or means; they are collaborators in a process whose end, unless you mean the obvious one, cannot be known at all.

266

It was once said that great poets steal, but, these days, writers wouldn't be so uncool as to get caught red-handed with even one of their own ideas.

267

Performing artists who are for ever donning a mask or disguise when young may be onto a good idea—but later, when they're more set in their ways, there'll be ones that fit less well and they'll only too evidently be trying it on.

268

It really is shameful and humiliating to think that you might be writing to solicit attention and maybe even love. Given that you have attention enough and love in a life, why then keep on producing and publishing? Either you're deeply habituated in this way of responding to a need that has now disappeared, or you've been motivated all along by something else entirely.

269

That's the second time today someone's said they envy me . . . Perhaps I'd be able to enjoy life more if I learned how to envy myself.

270

I have to admit that I'm at home practising a minority art. It's good, essential even, to be read—but I don't know what I'd do if read by everyone.

271

Occasionally, in a good light, it's possible to glimpse the sight of us all working on a collaborative text called: the people living now.

272

That 'well-written' is an adjective used by editors to damn with faint praise itself exemplifies the ill use English must nowadays endure.

273

Poets are farmers with a weather eye open on their own fallow fields.

274

The 'new' shamelessness: not only do the in-crowds who scratch each others' backs with grants, awards, and prizes give the entire way of life a bad name, they simultaneously work to poison the out-crowds with their own bile—and that *is* a shame.

275

Only a Ulysses with wax in his ears could possibly survive in this climate to hear himself think.

276

An anthology subtitled 'real poems for unreal times' looks as though it's making a stand. Yet since these times, however difficult, are no less real than any other, the gesture of defiance misfires—which is why it's the poems included that are besmirched with precisely the airs of just such a marketing ploy as gives these times their illusion of unreality.

277

Once I happened to reiterate the claim that poetry makes things happen by underlining its role in life, and so placing it alongside other human implements. My host replied that it's not then strictly the poetry that does the making ... In which case nothing in itself made by human beings makes anything happen either!

278

Still, we are tool-using creatures and the making things happen which goes on in human life also requires us to choose our instruments wisely. Pushkin, for example, might have been advised to stick with the poems and keep away from the duelling pistols.

279

As if just like the fact that Jesus can't be a Christian or Marx a Marxist, the one place I never feel wholly at home is home.

280

Newspapers should always be read a week or so late: that way you see more clearly what might have been worth reading.

281

People who find it difficult to see things from others' points of view will tend to assume they are immortal. How could there be a world without them in it?

282

The private view was crowded. Almost everyone was there, people propped against the walls or hanging on like hyperrealist sculptures. But one room was the art itself: a false, treated ceiling with skewered hardback books suspended on steel cables, and pressing down above the heads of drink-less revellers. What kind of private view was that? It was a claustrophobic culture's.

283

Those people who spend their time checking other people's clothes are usually too busy to notice that somebody else may be checking their behaviour.

284

Critics and editors have sometimes complained that the poetry I write violates some taboo distinction between public and private—but, surely, any mobile phone user regularly out-violates me.

285

Today I was in a bookshop, just browsing along the shelves, when a woman took out her mobile phone and made a call. The next thing I knew, she was reading poems into it, saying 'This is a good one …' 'It's by Pedro Salinas,' she was saying, 'What? No, Pedro Salinas!' I had heard of people phoning home to check that they're buying the right sort of cheese, but here was an impromptu public recitation, and for the apparent benefit of no one else present.

286

'But why are you crying?' she asked. 'Good question,' said the language teacher in me. 'I'm not: it's the tear duct on that side doesn't work, and what you see are artificial tears.' Yet wiping away that leakage, as they took up their listening exercise, I couldn't help thinking of possible answers to why the one dry eye in that classroom might have been prompted to weep—when, for example, happiness comes, but its price is just too high.

287

There's definitely one thing more alarming than a triumphalist politician: it's a soul-searching one.

288

You've seen them pacing about public spaces talking out loud to thin air. No, they're not raving lunatics or poets composing—they're just people chatting on a 'no handset' phone.

289

Every summer must be spoiled by something; we're lucky when it's only by the weather.

290

Post-modern authors: it may indeed be that they have nothing to say, but at least they exhaust their subject.

291

'You're a cynic' is the tribute paid by the deluded to a person whose innocence has been pickled in reality.

292

'Human kind / Cannot bear very much reality' is a phrase from someone who worked in a publisher's office. What's more, if it's true, then the fact of it is also a part of reality.

293

A number of our Italian friends are benign Anglophiliacs—blithely unaware that the disease has a virulent strain.

294

We're in a vicious circle? Perhaps. But, don't forget, the degree of the viciousness doesn't depend on the fact that we are in a circle.

295

You can't expect a kettle letting off steam to produce a convincing analysis of why it's boiling.

296

A prophylactic for splenetic writers, satirists, journalists, and everyone: your descriptions, don't forget, are always also of yourself.

297

It's all very well for there to be creative writing courses springing up everywhere, but where would they be without creative reading?

298

If ignorance were bliss, wouldn't the world be a happier place?

299

Sometimes it can feel as if people have gone out of fashion, but in fact that's wrong, they were never really in.

300

Yesterday I read an account of a confrontation at a conference when an Indian anthropologist criticized the British for destroying the practice of praying to a certain goddess for protection from smallpox—by introducing the use of vaccine among the subject population. A question from the floor asked if the suffering and death avoided didn't justify the cultural loss. The anthropologist wouldn't grant the point and instead attacked the cultural assumptions of western medicine, thus prompting an all-too-familiar academic deadlock. Yet from the viewpoint of cultural conservation, what makes it any less urgent to preserve the structuring assumptions of western medicine than those of an eastern religion? Cultural relativism cuts all ways. And what if the eastern goddess had answered the prayers of her worshippers, even to the extent of sacrificing her own cult, by temporarily using the British to bring some relief to her followers?

301

A writer boldly asserts of *The Divine Comedy* that Hell is the place where you are condemned to tell your story for eternity. Heaven, on the other hand, is where you will be allowed to forget it in exchange for taking on wisdom. But Dante would never have managed to complete his visit to all three places if he hadn't stuck to his story of needing to meet Beatrice just that one more time.

302

These days it's not difficult to identify analogies when reading the *Inferno*, but whatever could his *Purgatorio* and *Paradiso* correspond to now? (Or at any time, for that matter.)

303

The idea that only native speakers can understand a nation's literature is too often the response of privilege to a hard-working lack of franchise.

304

Even the spiritual is only human.

305

With soured friendships, failed love affairs, and marriages that end in divorce, it's the remnant of what was once held in common that inevitably proves the most aggravatingly contentious.

306

Lichtenberg writes that the truth will find a publisher at any time, but that complaisance will usually only do so for a year. Thus he recommends taking up the pen with courage and candour. Of course he's right in his conclusions, whatever the outcome, but would he be so sanguine about finding publishers if he were writing now?

307

We appear to be living in a culture in which to compare oneself with a great writer of the past—with an Austen or a Wordsworth—is automatically taken to be a symptom of presumption. Yet why is it not the sign of an egalitarianism expressed by means of a grateful respect for the achievements of the dead?

308

Nietzsche was afflicted not only by his genius, but also by a sense of his own worth.

309

You want to protect your reputation? Then you've already lost it.

310

On Nietzsche's sister and other hagiographers: whenever I encounter a 'keeper of the flame', instinctively I reach for my fire extinguisher.

311

If the resentment of the marginalized is pitiable because perhaps justified, that flaunted by the successful as a mark of their roots is both pitiful and pitiless.

312

What if the great difference between us and all the other sound-producing creatures were only that we have evolved ways of transcribing our sounds?

313

The mother tongue comes from the breast.

314

The unforgivable thing done to you is exactly what you must learn to forgive, because if you don't it will destroy you.

315

'Please forgive me, please forgive me,' she had begged. I did; but now, months later, it seems she can't forgive *me* for knowing this shameful thing about her.

316

It is a structural fact about aspirations to social improvement and the retention of power that left-liberal governments tend to be accused of hypocrisy and right-wing governments are not. The world might be a better place if it were the other way round—but then the world wouldn't need governing or governmental oversight either.

317

A week is a long time in poetry.

318

The problem with the opinion that an intellectually poor prime minister or president must be the puppet of a far cannier clique is that such a clique might well not want to be associated with a puppet that couldn't dance convincingly to a range of clever tunes.

319

Borges calls *Moby-Dick* 'a parable of the . . . wrong way of fighting evil'—which would make it a book only too relevant to our, or any, moment for that matter. And just how many will fail to survive that mad pursuit?

320

Calling your enemies 'evil' pays them the compliment of being apparently motivated by nothing so venal as mere self-interest or petty calculation. Naturally, you assume by this use of the word that, opposing the 'evil', you stand with the 'good'. Yet your all but compulsive reiterations of the word haplessly bespeak a familiarity with its ways that is only too often the result when paired evaluative terms are so depended on by a public speaker. But then how right you're proved! Your popularity rating goes up with the temperature of your speechifying. Which is how you fall victim to what can only seem your, or your party's, petty calculation.

321

You want to get rid of weapons of mass destruction? Why not start with the toxic dualisms in your own speechifying?

322

Sentimentality and violence always have been different sides of the same too hurriedly circulating coin.

323

Consumerism too has its fundamentalists.

324

How suitable for a possession-possessed era it is that '*Get* a life!' should have had its vogue in these years—as if the phrase could be hurled at anybody who wasn't already enduring one.

325

People with exclusive tastes will go slumming for variety; people with more varied ones don't need to demean themselves in such a fashion.

326

Mid-life crises: so tell me, where exactly does the *Via d'amore* turn into the *Viale delle rimembranze*?

327

One problem of my isolation from the society of native speakers is that I grow out of practice at speaking face to face with people who will understand me *only too well*.

328

Just as a warm thought amid a flurry of bitter ones fails to annul them, so too with a stab of envy that seems to taint good will and fellow feeling.

329

Somehow I would feel better about such publicity antics as a National Poetry Day if the celebrity poets involved were raising money for charities and not trying to prise a charitable response from a distracted public.

330

The Jeremiads of the moment are, by definition, unable to balance their scare- and fear-mongering against the vast range of ordered living which the daily tremors of the newsworthy require as a practically unreported background.

331

What looked like the final insult was the way in which an incorrigibly cynical corporate oligarchy would vitiate the art that protested against it, both through the bitterly mimetic damage in the art itself and through its purchases for the private collections of billionaires. But the notion that this might be the 'final insult' was far too optimistic.

332

Don't forget: the real decision to do without something must depend on the still felt presence of a strong desire for whatever it may have been you wanted, but couldn't have, or decided you'd be better off renouncing.

UNIVERSITY OF WINCHESTER LIBRARY

333

In an unfamiliar city, neither his nor mine, I had stepped down from a
tram onto an avenue that dwarfed us in a Moscow or Frankfurt of the
mind. He was somewhere ahead with his people, a critic or two, and I
was still young. We had gone into an institute and were climbing flights
of broad stone stairs which swept us up and around as they turned.
Introduced by one of those supporters, I had mumbled some words
of admiration. Then the old poet took me aside. At the deep ledge of
a window, though I didn't understand, there was something in his air,
something altogether familiar—which is how he let me know, just as
he seemed to have done those years before. Whatever it was that dream
conveyed, I really couldn't say, waking into a chilly bedroom alone and
some hours before dawn. Yet it didn't fade. There was no withdrawal
of the intimate sign, or so I keep telling myself, as a trace of it lingered
throughout the day.

334

Vittorio Sereni once said to me in a lift that the essential requirement
for a poet was patience. He had less than a year to live.

335

The poet's novel: needless to say, it's very well written, but it doesn't
think 'character is plot', or even that the characters in themselves are
either of much interest or importance ... It's a first person narrative.
Sadly, the character's too autobiographical, over-informed about far too
many things, and definitely not the kind of chap to have around in a
crisis. But the main flaw, if you'll allow me, is its total lack of any feel-
good factors—unless you happen to like writing, that is.

336

What's the best thing to do with a *roman à clef*? Throw away the key.

337

It's important to take part in the intellectual life of your own time—if only to salute those ideas about to die.

338

He was one of those people who are difficult to fathom because they have no depths.

339

My style? When young I got used to vamping on an upright piano with the mute pedal permanently down.

340

But being an artist *is* like watching paint dry.

341

Human conditions: science may have altered the circumstances, but it hasn't touched the terms.

342

There are times when falling between two stools may be the only way to keep out of the shit.

343

It's a mistake for politicians to claim the moral high ground: they can never apply their ethical stances across the board; so their virtuous absolutes look conditioned by pragmatism and national interest (as they almost inevitably are). Then the charge of hypocrisy, however unfair, follows by return of post.

344

The only decent way to honour your war dead is to find means for resolving any conflict without adding to them.

345

Finally I realized what had been irritating me about a much younger colleague: I was resenting her assumption that everything will always work out in just the way she wants it to.

346

People think it's our job to keep up standards, and they're right. If you have high standards of flexibility and insightfulness you won't sound and behave like a moral oaf.

347

I've been accused of running down my friends behind their backs. Yet being too concerned about what people think of you will prevent being truthful about your sense either of them or anything else we care to mention.

348

Once upon a time, understanding something meant seeing it in the best light that your culture could cast; but such a light would also inevitably produce a long and deep back shadow. Nowadays, understanding requires the use of multiple lights placed at various angles created by the distinct and relevant cultural identities of the world's populations. Though the state of things now absolutely requires this, very few—and hardly any of the nationally powerful, it would seem—look like they're in a position to appreciate the greater illumination generated by multiple light sources. Perhaps this is one reason why even the few glimpses of understanding we are granted also serve to underline a chronic loneliness.

349

Beauty can't be in the eye of the beholder. To see is to process optical data. The processing has to be learnt. Beauty is a shared understanding that will, or will not, be passed on to future generations.

350

It's important to have your emotions, e.g. by reflecting on them; otherwise, they'll have you.

351

Perhaps it's better to play fast and loose with opinions: you'll doubtless find it useful to *have* them, but don't necessarily need to *hold* them.

352

Asked after a lecture why he had said that a rhyme was bad, a distinguished literary critic was heard to offer this one-word reply: 'Taste.' He then twisted the knife by immediately adding, 'Next question.' Could he really have been unaware that *accounting for taste* is the one thing that separates him from the philistines who don't know much about art but know what they like?

353

People who think they can't change are plainly the ones who need to most.

354

But the writer is a dogged snail.

355

In any evolving pattern or series it's the elements that appear not to fit which will prove the most significant.

356

Stockhausen's idea that a successful terrorist attack widely watched on television screens could be a work of art recalls Walter Benjamin on the Futurists. They are the apotheosis of *l'art pour l'art* because they offer the prospect of our own destruction as an aesthetic spectacle. Which is to say (I've always supposed) that if terrorist outrages and Futurism are both art, well then, they're bad art.

357

Absolute power over life and death, like that of the Roman Emperor at the end of a gladiatorial contest, can never be art—because the omnipotence, being a matter of personal whim, has no meaning. And this applies to novelists who, approaching the one by killing off a character for the convenience of the plot, simultaneously distance their work from the other.

358

I'm in Santander again, walking with a group of acquaintances across a large grassed square in the middle of town. Ornate churches and other civic edifices are all around us. I'm discussing how the place has a curiously English character, and we agree that it results from centuries of trade between the two countries. It feels good to be back here again, though I don't know where we're heading or exactly what I'm here for. Yes, it certainly feels good—which is odd indeed because, awake, I've never set foot in the place.

359

Reading a poem for the first time is like trying to get money out of an ATM machine when you don't know the state of your account. Now and then the transaction is concluded with a cheering surprise.

360

Small presses tend to utter currency whose value can—at that moment—barely be traded on the money markets. Big presses haplessly issue junk bonds.

361

To the Zen sentence that if you meet the Buddha on the road, kill him, a Nietzsche might reply, if you meet God on the road, just give him a smile. It must be a case of mistaken identity. The poor fellow will be suffering from delusions of grandeur.

362

'The Silent Channel', a poem with no words dedicated to the memory of Karl Kraus, and with the following epigraph: 'Entspannen Sie sich—auf diesem Kanal werden alle Nebengeräusche gedämpft' ['For absolute silence we have created this noiseless channel so you can relax without being disturbed.]' *Austrian Airlines.*

363

A politically correct culture is an imitation fur coat—inhabited by real fleas.

364

'I wouldn't trust my memory as far as I could throw it.' 'So how far would that be?' 'Sorry?'

365

Not only do some people want to talk you to death, they want to do the post-mortem as well.

366

Progress: it's as if we had fashioned a stick to help a poor man walk, and then obliged him to do nothing but feign a worsened hobble.

367

'Normal service will be resumed as soon as possible' (official stamp on a birth certificate).

368

'A pure heart is an excellent thing,' Lichtenberg wrote, 'and so is a clean shirt.' Oh if only I could take my heart to the cleaners!

369

Old-time eroticism: the more you cover, the more there is to discover. Contemporary eroticism: even our fig leaves are peek-a-boo.

370

A home truth from a political commentator discussing red tape and bureaucracy in the European Union: '. . . the British people don't need any more literature.'

371

Whenever I hear a security announcement asking me to report anything that looks suspicious, suddenly *everything* does.

372

Foreignness is its own reward.

373

It happens that I can't re-read a novel that I know I like. Even a sentence or two just produces a nauseous vertigo. But it's not the book I can't stand to revisit. It's the person who used to like it that's making someone feel faintly sick.

374

Wittgenstein makes much of the fact that his right hand could not give his left hand some money. Yet by far the hardest debts to repay are the ones you incur with yourself.

375

Recognition is the status that a society's representatives confer on an artist. If and when it comes, the thing will likely feel decidedly hollow. Not so the appreciation that you may receive from an individual reader.

376

Even de-contextualization has to take place *somewhere.*

377

The number of how-to-do-it manuals there are for poetry in bookshops these days, you'd think it was the new sex.

378

Come to think of it, the relations between meter and rhythm are not so unlike those between sex and love.

379

All this branding of others as elitists is enough to make you die of loneliness. Try to tell someone you're just like everybody else, and they'll like as not banish you immediately to the fourth estate.

380

Some people need to have enemies—so as to be on their side as well.

381

Even if it were possible to 'know your own mind', I can't help thinking that the better policy would be to change it for the larger by means of curiosity and reflection.

382

Life so often seems like a play in which the characters are even less plausible than the backdrop—and that's precisely what makes them real.

383

Are intellectuals who—like Theodor Adorno—demonstrate the collusion between knowledge and power inevitably doomed to become authorities?

384

'JE est un autre': it's a curious fact that because we hear our voices through the bones of the skull, and are surprised by the recorded sounds we've made, the one person who can't hear his or her 'voice' as others will is the composing poet. Ah yes; but the poet's voice—being a style evolved through dialogues between writing, speaking, and listening as if you were another—is the audible structure of a particular poem played back through the poet's necessarily personal sound system. This is a reason, among many, why a poet's ear must be trained to hear the timbre of the language, and not have it drowned out by the sound of her or his own voice.

385

Where's the need of metaphysics when the wind is in the trees?

386

Those who imagine the verbal arts to be immaterial are not only forgetting the etymology of the word 'pen', the ingredients of 'ink', or the sound of wind through trees, they are overlooking all we owe to the force of gravity and to the earth's atmosphere.

387

Self-promoting authors must be volunteering to become canon-fodder.

388

You use your phone card. A voice comes on the line and asks you to put in your PIN number. You know it's a recording (each time you use the card it's exactly the same voice). Yet you find it impossible not to treat this voice-trace as a person talking to you. Do it about ten times in a row, and he or she may well start to sound irritated with you for pestering them so.

389

It is bred into us from our earliest times that words are traces of human presence, and to understand them we must actively engage with the reasons and purposes of that human presence in its communicative instant. That's what I try to do when reading a poem.

390

To assert that poets *can* be called upon to make a stand in times of crisis but not their poems, a writer draws an analogy between poets and carpenters. True, you can't expect a table to make a stand. Yet if it doesn't stand up at the moment the parties are sitting down to sign an accord, both furniture and carpenter have failed us.

391

Enduring solitude may be tough, but living with your self is tougher.

392

It's been said that 'formalist criticism wants to make itself unnecessary; historicist criticism, to make itself indispensable'. Yet, whatever it wants, in practice formalists tend to interpose themselves between processes of composition and natural reading, while, if historicists aren't at least as good close-readers as formalists, their findings will be not only unnecessary, but also irrelevant.

393

Formalist critics are forever in danger of writing like poets *manqués:* they make the mistake of thinking that you can show how a watch is put together by dismantling it.

394

It's been said by a young poet that nothing stimulates composition like the assurance that what you write will be published. Doubtless true, but when you have a bibliography, nothing suggests better that you've written something worth publishing than the fear that it won't be.

395

In two party systems—political or not—contrasts that valorize one of a symbiotic pair by trivializing the image of the supposedly only alternative promulgate the very thinness of cultural vision that they credit themselves with striving to combat.

396

Morality requires energy. Tired people fall into vice.

397

Among the problems for a writer with an ironic style, one that maintains its position by incorporating criticisms so as to disarm them, is that you have relieved yourself of the need to take any such criticisms seriously.

398

Whatever happened to the rise of the leisure classes? Our houses are filled with labour-saving devices, and yet no one has a moment to think.

399

So what's wrong with theoretical arguments in support of editorial decisions? When deciding what to accept and what reject for an issue of our poetry magazine, we would readily compromise on the work of a well-known writer, but argue interminably over the aesthetic merits of an obscure one.

400

How to mitigate the habit of binary thinking: take any pair of opposed terms (health and sickness, good and evil, right and wrong). Imagine them as points in space at the limits of your visual field, the one to the left, the other to the right; then draw a line joining the two. Now, consider the infinite number of points on that line which exist as neither the one nor the other; or, alternatively, think of the line as a sliding volume control—so much more useful for hearing the music than working with only an on-off switch.

401

Let's also try to get beyond the structuring contrast of 'the same' and 'the different'—because while the former colonizes, the latter alienates. Similarity and difference, too, have to be interdependent states of relative understanding.

402

Monopolizing one emotion in art is the most direct route to being first pigeonholed, then shelved.

403

The weakness of anger as an inspiration for art is that its natural instrument is a blunt one.

404

Being generous to someone who reviews you badly is a most nuanced form of tit-for-tat.

405

Galling as it is to hear yourself, your profession or vocation, run down to provide the setting for someone else's contrasted self-esteem, at least you can console yourself with the thought that—for this very same person—you're fulfilling a useful role in society.

406

It's been said, aphoristically, that aphorisms are aphids on the rose bush of literature. So what would that make the thorns? In nature and so—the analogy implies—in art, you can't have the roses without their parasitical and their protective devices.

407

If the beautiful wisteria is strangling the tree, that's how it is meant to be in nature.

408

But in art only time will tell who or what are the hosts, who or what the parasites.

409

The commercialization of sexuality is no more evident than in plucked, shaped, or shaven pubic hair: what was once virgin forest, now an environmental hot spot.

410

We had reached a point with the exploitation of travesty, parody, and pastiche where the only indirection left was to play it straight.

411

It's best to accept honest gifts with all the grace you can muster. After all, it may well be better to give than to receive, but if there were nobody here to receive, how then could anyone be better by giving?

412

Marinetti: Toad of Toad Hall without the charm.

413

Though it's right enough to scold your children when they tell a lie, secretly you can be at least a little proud of them. They've evidently taken one more step in forming both a private and a social identity.

414

'Face value' sounds as if it must mean 'not the actual value'.

415

Literary criticism could at least aspire to be the grain of sand in the oyster shell.

416

Revising a work of art is like arriving at a point in a road where it suddenly gives out into not even a dirt track. In order to make the next step, you have to imagine an intersection with innumerable exit roads, then imagine a signpost, and then decide what is the best road to take so as to get to a destination that you will only recognize when you have arrived there.

417

The object itself can suggest, but can't tell you, how it should be revised—and nor can a set of theoretical precepts about what you want or mean to do with this piece of art. The tradition in which you are working is no more than a code word for a habituated imagining of intersections, exit roads, signposts, and, only up to a point, what might be the best turn to make in these unique circumstances.

418

The limit in how far a tradition can help you in writing or revising is set by the fact that, as well as trying to finish your work, you must also be trying to add something to that tradition.

419

Poets have to serve so many masters that they're likely to lose track, which is doubtless how they become their own master.

420

There's nothing wrong with acting like a prima donna—just so long as you happen to be the best girl in the troupe.

421

Good poets don't 'come down hard' on stressed syllables (because no one does). We rise into stressed syllables by lengthening the vowel and *raising* the pitch. It's only when parodying the pronunciation to bring out the 'metrical pattern' that we 'come down hard'. And this may be one of the differences between the thump of verse and the rhythm of poetry.

422

While the only way to discover our own limits is to push against where we think they may be to see if they 'give', the only way to discover others' limits is to try and describe, with all the generosity available, the points where 'give' gives out.

423

Yet don't forget, if, to recall Wilde, critics are artists, the appreciation of others' limits must be one way they discover—by pushing up against them—their very own.

424

The society of dead poets: the natural tendency may well be to etherealize them so as more easily to facilitate their apotheosis. But we should lend them the bodies they no longer have, bring their works to life as human products, and, back down on earth, try to remember them exactly as they were.

425

Just because you don't happen to be top dog doesn't mean you can't allow yourself to bark and chase sticks at all.

426

The world's not driven by the marketplace, but by the idea of the marketplace. It isn't so much sales figures that make people jump; it's the thought of future sales.

427

Last night I dreamed that a poem of mine had been accepted for publication by a newspaper of some kind. The poem was called 'The Statue'. If only I'd corrected a proof in the dream, then I could at least have tried to write it come the morning.

428

An ever-present temptation for prophets is the wish tacitly to collaborate in bringing about the disasters they foresee.

429

If you attempt the impossible, when unsuccessful, have you failed?

430

The best things in life may be free, but the good things tend to come fairly expensive.

431

Much as I love painting, one of the things that decided me between it and poetry when young was the modesty of means required to practise the latter. Even now in a gallery or when flicking through an issue of *Art News*, I can be turned away entirely by the colour of money.

432

The stoics may not be able to help you face death, but they can surely do something with the thought of facing it.

433

A theorist of post-historical art history praises art for involving a spectator over technology that requires a user. Fair enough! Well said! But that Kantian note about art and its disinterested contemplation rather deflates such grand theories about how nowadays things have utterly changed . . . and as any decent artist is likely to tell you, looking at something is a way of using it.

434

One difficulty with the life of exile in a strange land is that you must survive as an inner emigré as well.

435

We have entered a new era in world history (which is to say we're being obliged to fear a new set of enemies).

436

Wallace Stevens wrote in 1942 that 'There is no distance' because he could lie in bed in Hartford, Connecticut, and hear a radio broadcast from Cairo. But rapidity of electronic communication has not abolished our sense of material distance. If anything, it has increased it.

437

Why is some artists' early work so much more appealing and attractive than their mature achievement? Is it because the marks of uncertainty and exploration are also traced with the desire to please and to make a mark? Or is it that people simply find it easier to identify with that searching for a definite direction and to patronize it? Compare the ways in which biographies of writers and artists tend to grow dull when headlines spin and success arrives.

438

Ambition is what people of limited talent use for motivation.

439

If Milton should be living at this hour, and fame really were the spur, then he'd have gone blind in the entertainment industry. And yet once more, o ye laurels: heaven cannot be a spiritual Oscar ceremony in the sky.

440

Suddenly I found myself remembering that when a boy the mysterious other, the Orient, if you will, began at Calais . . . or maybe even Birmingham.

441

You may be your own worst enemy, but try not to be everyone else's too.

442

You work to make amends; but there's only so much you can do, and soon the self-humiliation takes its toll on everyone.

443

When Wilde wrote that there's no such thing as a moral or an immoral book, there are only well- or badly-written ones—he doubtless had *The Bible* in mind.

444

The best jokes are the unintended ones. A depressed old man at a therapy session in Haverhill, Suffolk, run by my first wife, a session otherwise attended by depressed women, was being recommended to keep active by doing some light housework. 'But there are no lighthouses in Haverhill,' he replied.

445

While an unreserved surrender to the world and its ways will likely consort with what's called evil, so too will a dogmatic denial of the same world's inevitable realities.

446

As it says, the first shall be last and the last shall be first. Perhaps even the pro-life lobby will wake up one day to find that it hasn't been what it assumed itself to be.

447

Hofmannsthal wrote that living people differ from fictitious characters to the extent that the latter are given coherence and inner unity by their creators where the former are bundles of incoherence held together by physical existence. This, doubtless, helps to explain why making your characters resemble real people invites having them pronounced unbelievable.

448

It's perfectly possible for nettled egalitarians to be ashamed of their own distinction.

449

To hear the Christian Fundamentalists talk you'd think they were born again yesterday.

450

To all those who claim to be doing God's will on earth, I say—certainly you are; but you do believe he works in a mysterious way? What if he

UNIVERSITY OF WINCHESTER LIBRARY

were merely using you to thwart your preferred end, as a means to punishing your very presumption in claiming to be doing his will?

451

Taking issue with others' pronouncements without being understanding of why they made them, you may win your arguments—but you won't convince anyone of anything more than, at best, your display of rectitude.

452

Have I ever quite spelled out in writings on poetry and circumstances that the one thing you must never ever do, as a poet or human being, is capitulate to them? After all, it's only through a resistance to circumstances that you can feel yourself to be thoroughly in them. Then again, don't forget, we are all of us someone else's circumstances too.

453

Writing and publishing books may allow you to feel a sense of fulfillment; but don't expect it to provide, or substitute for, either happiness or contentment.

454

Poets' lines must have marginal interest, both left and right. If not, their poems will have no more than marginal interest.

455

Post-modern conditions, as it were, yet once more: to be able to enjoy your life as a third-hand make-believe without the least shadow of shame at the pretence.

456

It may well be true, as Wilde wrote, that 'most people are other people' meaning that 'their thoughts are someone else's opinions, their life a mimicry, their passions a quotation'; but each of us, whoever we are, has no choice but to live our lives as if they were our own.

457

In the longer run, you may find that it's better to be good at something than to be right about it.

458

Encouraging others, by example, will likely take some courage.

459

If there's one thing more vulgar than vulgarity, it must surely be calling others vulgar.

460

Try your best to forgive everything—even your own dreadful lack of forgiveness.

461

Attachment to places in their own terms is a form of spiritual release.

462

Set the bar of best practice too high and you'll oblige truth to thrive in the black economy.

463

'I've completed my book' and 'I've lost my keys' have exactly the same grammatical form, though one is a verbal action that must be intended, while the other by definition can't be. Could this help explain why we may feel responsible for, and guilty about, happenings that we didn't and couldn't possibly intend?

464

'How would you source a creative writing programme?' I was asked in the course of a job interview. For a moment my mind leaped to pencils and paper, computers and printers. 'Do you mean people?' I found myself saying. 'I suppose I do,' came back the reply.

465

A charm offensive: an offensive charm.

466

The achievement in paying a compliment: neither flattery nor condescension, you offer without any need for return, and you underline equality between giver and receiver. What's more, you say something you believe to be true, and that you feel sure will prove a help or reassurance to the person with whom you are talking. I fear that there can't be enough compliments paid in the world.

467

Just as the unconscious proved to be a repository of sexual banalities, so the irrational element in poetry turned out to be ever so strangely predictable.

468

There may be no such thing as a free lunch; but no one with any dignity could think that picking up the tab means acquiring the person you're paying for too.

469

So what if the cold eyed have a point in assuming that there is only power and the will to power? The more it's true, the more the need for consensual rules to civilize those who wield it.

470

They that have power to hurt: the only mature power comes with the capacity and opportunity not merely to hold power to hurt in reserve, but never to need to use it at all.

471

One of literary criticism's more shameless moves is to construe principled decisions not to write in a certain fashion as phobic evasions of a feared (and thus valorized) other.

472

The Laodicean: in a conflicted world all sides want you either to be for them or against them. Yet, in that same world, it's likely you'll only be able to continue if spat out of all their mouths.

473

A literary critic and poet recently asked me what I thought was unique about my work. Well, I too can row a scull and ride a bike; but what I can't do is shout comments from the towpath through a megaphone at an oarsman when I'm the one sitting in the boat.

474

Stock markets fluctuate in response broadly to two kinds of news: sound performance analyses and predictions, or speculations based on such reports and in reaction to how other traders are speculating in the light of them. You'd have thought that literary critics would aim to provide sound analyses, but so often it turns out they're speeding up the circulation of rumour and repute.

475

The unreliability of literary scholars' evaluations can be predicted in inverse proportion to their investments of time and effort in their subjects. Still, people who haven't committed themselves to a subject are unlikely to be right about it either.

476

In art and literature, ethnicity counts for nothing—acculturation for everything. Perhaps so, but even in our fast-migrating world the separation between the ethnic origin and cultural development of an individual can hardly ever be considered total. Worse still, into this nest of difficulties for writers and others some cuckoos have granted themselves the task of issuing passports.

477

How odd that 'friendship, love and creation' should be described by an interviewer as 'props' that the interviewed poet is 'left with' in his alleged epistemological predicament. It's as if the finest of human achievements were no more than some bric-a-brac to facilitate bits of stage business in the play that is our lives.

478

People from other cultures may well appear curiously weightless. Couldn't that be because you are in no position to appreciate properly how weight is distributed where they live?

479

Art as alienation: just as a readymade cunningly thieves from daily life an ordinary response to useful objects, so the (said to be indefinable) Duchampian concept of the '*inframince*' cleverly privileges a niceness of perception and discrimination employed by visual artists, musicians, poets, house-cleaners, medical orderlies, and indeed any skilled craftsperson, on a daily basis.

480

Two young people ride past you in the street. Where are they going? In their style, already faintly dated, you sense the ghost-like fragility of youth. Ah yes, but they don't even notice you at all.

481

What a pity that the various overseas councils, centers, and institutes feel obliged to promote their own national cultures! That's what makes it so difficult for them to appear generously indebted to anything beyond their own borders. What's more, it promotes a national identity verging on, or tumbling into, a pretty poor self-parody.

482

Working in a demoralized and demoralizing atmosphere, you may well find it difficult to keep your morals intact.

483

The clever talk in paradoxes so as to impress. The wise speak in parable so as to be understood. Paradoxes, like jokes, are readily decoded. Parables prove tricky to interpret. This may be one reason why the clever can bank on a more immediate social success than the wise.

484

It's people and their fears that most frighten me about the future of the world.

485

Are all occasioned art works—and not just the evidently political protests—vulnerable to an accusation of dancing to others' agendas? Maybe they are, but only God creates out of a void.

486

The unexamined life is not worth living. The over-examined life is unendurable.

487

Whenever you encounter a distinction, rewrite it as a complex sentence.

488

Richard Rorty's pathos: the philosopher, in Hegel's words, aspires to 'hold his time in thought'—but what if his time, as in Warhol's slogan, turns out to be just fifteen minutes?

489

Academic specialists: mimics who don't even do their own voices.

490

Dealing with some publishers, it's only too easy to feel like a smuggler engaged in transporting contraband of no evident value across an iron curtain.

491

Superstition: a tribute paid by magical thinking to the randomness of things.

492

Pragmatism dissolves many of life's and philosophy's hard conundrums by asking the 'is it helpful for us to think this?' question. It can create an all but problem-free zone. Yet human life is by no means a problem-free zone—which is why the common sense of the pragmatist can prove as good as a fool's paradise.

493

Wagering on the existence of a divinity, or making a leap of faith … do either of these acts resemble devotional behaviour?

494

Despite all the paradoxes of so-called negative theology, and the divine as humanly unimaginable, I'm still left with the niggling suspicion that a vastly reassuring nothingness beyond our lives has been colonized and stratified by the enormously worldly empires of the Church.

495

If there's one thing worse than a gamekeeper condescending to a poacher, it's a gamekeeper who wants to pass himself off as a poacher. Not to worry, though: neither of these impertinences will have much bearing on us, their prey.

496

Pity the powerful in their power. Benighted and tired, they need understanding—and that's what they demand.

497

The task of poets is to inherit as much of their traditions as they are humanly able, extend them by cross-pollination from all the other cultures to which they can gain some access, and then hurl the results with all their might into whatever future may follow.

498

The difference between those who can't bring themselves to say 'thank you' to anyone and those who can't apologize to their social inferiors is that where the former lack the grace and insight to acknowledge the indebtedness they nevertheless sense, the latter are insufficiently secure in their social power to be able to grant that it too has limits not imposed from above. What marries them to each other is a pair of identities insufficiently strong to admit of evident weaknesses.

499

Where's the difference between my father's Christian providence (his belief that, however bad the occurrence, some good must come of it) and Nietzsche's idea that good is produced by evil?

500

Identity politics: life's conflicts may appear to reinforce identity by the re-assertive reactions of self-definition when under attack; but the courses of such conflicts in themselves will only too likely break up the grounds for those identities through loss, dismay, and self-parody-like propaganda.

501

One way beyond cultural relativism is to ask yourself how any particular community, and your own, addresses the tasks required for its continued existence. Then consider, with sympathy, its successes and failures.

502

The self-made are only too prone to behave in ways unpredictable to themselves and others. The real sources of their characters are what they most desire to be overlooked by other people and, it should surprise no one, by they themselves as well.

503

The benefits in reading translations shouldn't be sabotaged by being mistaken for the supposed gains in 'encountering foreignness'. They come from developing the habit of living with multiple perspectives, and are hard to distinguish in kind from learning languages, travelling, talking to people, or simply reading widely.

504

Only the creative can achieve real change, and the supercession of the past. The destructive provoke rebuilding programmes.

UNIVERSITY OF WINCHESTER LIBRARY

505

Le mot juste: consider the different relations between a sense of inevitability and necessity created, above all, by the nature of a rhythm, though reinforced and straitened by syntax and context, and a more broadly cultural sense of freedom and creative choice (the *mot juste* as the best selection from the possibilities). By contrast, consider the stymied feeling when a draft offers nothing but one necessary direction for development, and that one already known. The work dies in a desert of non-variables. Where there is no possibility, no uncertainty, and hence no unpredictability of outcome, there can be no creativity. Then the *mot juste* may not be strictly a creative conception, but rather a bit of post-facto preening in the artist, or backslapping on the part of a well-disposed critic.

506

If God's ways are unimaginable, then he's no earthly good to us.

507

The omnipotence of divinity precludes relationship: hence the loneliness of Protestants.

508

Religion is what we believe; superstition is what they believe. Dissolve that prejudice and sectarian strife goes with it. Ah, but where then would your leverage over the faithful be? Where your worldly power?

509

Overwhelmingly not quite convincing: someone trying to flatter, to seduce, or impress you.

510

Nietzsche's 'eternal recurrence': the Divine Will relocated in an individual fate.

511

The anecdotal method in poetry and elsewhere: what happened willy-nilly, and as an example of life being various, happened most importantly to *me*.

512

They say poetry is the Cinderella of the arts, and we all know what to expect if you get involved with her … you'll live happily ever after in a great big castle on a hill.

513

How fortunate that my anger may be construed as resentment! It can thus have no bearing on your behaviour, and obliges me miserably to amend mine.

514

Jaundiced and droopy, with thoughts of fall already, how the maples move.

515

Idealism takes some beating.

516

As if Adorno were actually recommending that no poetry be written after Auschwitz, pessimistic analyses of cultural collapse, of barbarism, or merely of dumbing down haplessly collaborate with the conditions they powerfully illuminate.

517

In a poetic culture where few risk being anything so un-cool as 'heavy', the punch lines of poems don't tend even to be bantam weight ones.

518

More unjust pity: the hapless pathos of deposed leaders on trial for war crimes.

519

If looks could kill, we would all be on death row for first-degree murder.

520

Strong poets? Good poets need to be strong enough not to over-defend their work against the strengths that derive from its weaknesses.

521

Negatively capable poets try to have the courage of their lack of convictions.

522

In a world where self-interest is the rule, generosity must pay twice (in kind and in cash)—but that is its reward.

523

Those who think they can solve life's problems by avoiding anything but commercial relations with others do no more than oblige people to have other than commercial relations with them.

524

Book sales are summed up. Readers count as singularities, one after another.

525

The worst kinds of believers are the ones who think they can do some insider trading with their God.

526

Is omnipotence in the same predicament as complete powerlessness? Hardly. Yet what a believer might find reassuring about God is that he's incapable of letting you down.

527

Poor old northern realism: it's just too true to be good!

528

Certainly you can't live in a work of art, and you'd be perverse to try; but you can live by art, and while working at the latter you well may find yourself immersed in it.

529

Yes, you can be immersed in art, but preferably not your own work. Sensible artists remain something of a stranger in that extent-less other country.

530

You can take a holiday from your life, but not from your mortality.

531

The great thing about thinking you have something which needs to be expressed is that it generates technical problems. Solve the problems and you will have squeezed out, one way or another, whatever there might have been to express. The realization as to which kind of squeezing has taken place will emerge in its own good time.

532

The painter Gerhard Richter writes that 'nature . . . knows no meaning', then that 'every beauty that we see in landscape . . . is our projection' and finally that 'we can switch it off at a moment's notice, to reveal only the appalling horror and ugliness.' But if the first of these statements is true, then nature without our projections would have to be meaningless: 'appalling horror and ugliness' sounds very like one of our projections to me.

533

Helping a blind man into a video rental store the other day—I found that strangely reassuring.

534

'Maastrict / was the Waterloo we lost, a diplomatic / Austerlitz' writes a distinguished British poet with internationalist credentials—only serving to prove how, among other things, the point Heraclitus made about rivers can be applied to history too.

535

As far as British, and other, poetry is concerned, the issue is no longer whether a poet has travelled or stayed at home, but whether any of them has got beyond the idea of 'abroad'.

536

You'll know you're starting to find yourself when you no longer recognize any of the circumambient signposts or signs.

537

Loneliness is a window tax on being, feeling yourself to be, or being forced to admit you are, unique.

538

In the last century efforts were made by ideologies in conflict to exile the mass of humanity from any private life at all, or, conversely, from any public life at all. Both of these extremes constitute tyranny—and each in the name of the people. So it may be that the possibility of osmosis between public and private is what most troubles the orders of social control . . . and among the most truth-bearing forms of barely-noticed movement back and forth through that membrane is, if you'll allow me, unfashionable poetry.

539

Bonjour, Monsieur Courbet: three realist studio figures and a dog rendered oddly unreal by being transported to a Hollywood-backdrop outdoors, which includes a freely-sketched, anecdotally departing coach . . . But even so you'll never get anywhere in the understanding of art if you won't go at least halfway to meet it.

540

Poetry critics who can't discuss techniques are as good as tongue-tied by their examples' own compacted eloquence.

541

It may be true that poets compound and critics expound; but poets also have to occasion their enigma variations, while critics can't be explaining all *ad infinitum*.

542

Half the problem with the hyphenated compound 'poet-critic' is that the first part is an honorific, but the second's a job description. The other half is that the honorific skews the job description, which, in turn, denies the honorific.

543

At the ends of wars you may have defeated your enemies, but beware of surprise attacks from your still unconquered need for them.

544

One drawback with 'the given' is that it gets 'taken for granted'.

545

'Il sonno ha similitudine colla morte' . . . but Leonardo is wrong: sleep doesn't resemble death. In the former, a person is present; in the latter, the person is not   and it shows.

546

The exile's fear of repatriation: if it's one thing to be shipwrecked on a desert island, it's another to be shipwrecked back home.

547

A limit to dreaming: things can happen in my dreams, and I can plan things in them; but the things that I plan in my dreams can't, it seems, happen—even in my dreams . . . and the threat that they might is enough to waken me.

548

The assertion that there *is* more than one world, supported by the banal fact that the word can be used in the plural or that someone or other may be 'in a world of his own', that's nothing less than the hubris of subjectivity and representation.

549

Whatever it is, if it is, the Beyond cannot be a 'world' in any sense we may understand by that word. An honest religious feeling for life is born with the recognition that belief in another world beyond the world is properly groundless.

550

We don't, because we can't, live in our own minds.

551

The reason why individual consciousnesses are not worlds is because they can be inhabited neither by others, nor by the one of whose consciousness it is. Stand in a crowd at a public gathering of any kind and imagine the extent to which your existence is registered by the minds of those around you. Equally, to what extent do any of those others impinge on or take up residence in yours? Few of us ever consider our existence in the minds of others. If our life depended on their thought of us, we would immediately cease to exist.

552

The language of poetry in our time is necessarily intimate. Your true readership, however large or small, forms an extended family.

553

A Japanese student told me the other day that she felt sorry for Jesus on the Cross. Why are Christians not usually taught, or not allowed, to feel, or express such an apparently natural sentiment? If we felt sorry for him, he couldn't be the Son of God.

554

Intelligent design? We could certainly do with more of it.

555

I hear a critic noting with reason that even the best poets only manage to write a few great poems. Yet art is a way of life, and our task is not only the production of flawless pearls for connoisseurs.

556

Is that what we want, the pursuit of happiness? Isn't it rather the pursuit of meaningfulness?

557

It's an achievement to be forgotten. Most of us are barely ever even called to mind.

558

Persons in a crowd: the more of them there are, the less humanity you feel.

559

Why are people always getting in my way? It must be because I can't get out of theirs.

560

The psychopathology of everyday life: why when trying to remember the name of a mutual acquaintance do I so often find myself calling her or him, embarrassingly, by the name of the person to whom I am talking? Whatever the reason, my embarrassment stems from having appeared to allow my interlocutor a momentary glimpse of how interchangeably they figure in my inner address and phone book.

561

Is it really impossible for artists to have the sorts of sustaining relationship with their own work that they can have with that of others? I do understand why this might be, since the psychology and perspective in the relationship is so different. Yet if it is true, it's saddening or only partially so, because, after all, it is possible for artists to feel satisfaction in what they have done, even if, the work being completed, it also leaves them both detached and curiously indifferent or empty.

562

Back in Cambridge, years ago, some people would sometimes refer to my then wife and I as an *ideal* couple. I should have known from their use of that word there was something dreadfully wrong . . . and not only with us.

563

What I like about the future is that it's made of words.

564

The problem with the narrative evaluation of a life, a philosopher friend tells me, is that our stories edit out the uncomfortably inconsistent or incoherent details—the confusions in us that smack of the truth and which categorically distinguish us from characters in a novel. Yet how would it be if we edit these out not because we want to conceal the lumpy truth from ourselves or others, but because we want to spare others a blurted out glimpse of those very sordid or pitiful or embarrassedly self-pitying details?

565

After all, about the incoherent inner detail that we haplessly or inadvertently reveal to the perceptive, there's little or nothing any one of us can do.

566

My blind spots about myself, invisible to me as they by definition are, may be, nevertheless, what others' behaviour in my vicinity allows me momentarily to glimpse.

567

One of my oldest friends once wanted to write a short story in which it was slowly revealed to the central protagonist that what he didn't like about other people was the effect his presence had upon them.

568

How much easier it is to pronounce on the sexual mores of society when your libido is waning and your choices (for better or worse, for richer or poorer) have long been made.

569

The strength of mind gained through a recognition of how fragile are the grounds on which others hopes and joys must be founded is instantly lost through the display of even the slightest superiority over them—for to be disillusioned with humanity shows how weak is the ground upon which you yourself must be standing.

570

It's only the really good teams who can consistently get results without home advantage—and the same is true of scholars when not on their own field.

571

A poet whose work means a lot to me is criticized for not sufficiently cultivating the reader. Still, for some of us, there's nothing more off-putting than being relentlessly chatted up.

572

One more thing I owe to the English language: without it I wouldn't have the means for adopting a critical perspective on its own injustices of usage and abusage.

573

Write for the moment and the moment will swallow you whole.

574

Write *sub specie aeternitatis* and you'll find you have nowhere else to stand.

575

A Japanese architect at the heart of a scandal concerning earthquake resistance data has been found to have lied to a parliamentary committee examining the issue at which he appeared wearing an obvious and ill-fitting wig . . . His evidently shameful baldness was all too soon exposed as well.

576

As can be seen from the tensions flaring between players in close matches, the game of soccer appears to mirror a male frustration. It is so difficult to score; collaborations of the most elegant kind are wrecked by a timely lunge; fates of teams are decided by an arbitrary decision, a stroke of luck, or the exercise of a momentary and inspired improvisation . . . No wonder those elements among the supporters desperately in need of a release from their manifest frustrations, can take it out on the opposing fans, or, after losses, on anyone or anything unfortunate enough to get in their way.

577

Confessing you're self-centred hardly makes you less so.

578

Wounded *amour propre*, undiagnosed in fits of righteous anger, is only too likely to decline into a coarsened self-pity masquerading as grief at the spectacle of the world's unending sorrows and injustices.

579

One of the many fallacies sprung up like weeds in the environs of the idea that subjectivity can be attacked by noting that the meaning of a work is not limited to what was intended concerns the plain fact that while you can, and almost always will, use chance, random, or not wholly controlled, elements in the creation of a work of art, you cannot make art *by accident*.

580

While the most powerful and vociferous politicians and spokespersons for tribes and clans pit their own traditions against those of others, taking stances against mutual acknowledgements and innovations, the best artists see no contradiction in the innovative preservation of traditions which foster their meanings through the recognition and accommodation of significant differences between those same cultures and traditions.

581

The pen is mightier than the sword only in so far as it isn't used to divide and rule.

582

I have made an enemy: someone has over-identified himself with the imagined status that my vicinity appears to confer. Inevitably disappointed in my actual behaviour, he has recoiled from the supposed affront to his dignity—and now persecutes me, first behind my back and then to my face, as one whose precious friendship has been so presumptuously betrayed.

583

There is at least as much danger in over-identification with things as in disdaining them.

584

The formalism wars: Robert Frost wrote that free verse was like playing tennis without a net. Ah yes, but Ezra Pound could play a mean game of tennis.

585

Where would ironists be if no one took them seriously? That's why, so as to catch us unawares, they maintain such painfully straight faces.

Yet the irony is that this is just how they teach us not to take them seriously.

586

An Italian summer: every postage stamp of beach jam-packed with shame taking a vacation from itself.

587

Once we were obliged to be sickly, overworked and underfed. Now we're expected to be overweight, lobster-burned, compulsively consuming. The end is much the same. Only the means have changed.

588

They say that when you drown your whole life flashes before your eyes. But if you try and remember even a single event in all its detail, you'd have to wonder how it could.

589

Last night at dinner we were told a story about an anthology issue of a poetry magazine in which a criterion for inclusion was that the poet had to be dead. One over-ambitious soul proposed that he or she be included with a death date in the parenthesis—which, in the subsequent issue could be announced as an unfortunate mistake. Now that's what I call tempting fate!

590

Many an Italian application form begins with the request that you declare yourself to be still living. I wonder how many have lied when completing it?

UNIVERSITY OF WINCHESTER LIBRARY

591

Rule following and outward criteria: I see how it can be decisive in mathematics, language-use, social customs, etc—so as to manifest the difference between thinking you are following a rule and actually following one. Yet what about the difference between thinking you are doing the morally right thing, and actually doing it? There you have only your intuition, judgment, and experience to guide you.

592

Poor fellow, he was one of those writers who believed his own theories.

593

Talking to him was like trying to insert lines in a script he'd already learned by heart.

594

For a dedication: 'To the paparazzi of the soul'.

595

Taking your life may be the very last arrow in a passive-aggressive person's quiver. But just imagine to what you must have been driven when it feels there's no other choice but to loose and lose it.

599

Politicians who want to leave a mark on history tend to find they are making it with other people's blood.

600

And where, pray, is the tomb of the unknown civilian?

601

One of the hopes there is in the face of evil, coming from whatever quarter, must be in the fact that when evil miscalculates—as it surely will—good, from whatever quarter, may find itself offered an opening.

602

Poems need to be caught at a medium airspeed: take them too fast and they form no trace; fly too slow and you stall.

603

A simple rhyme: success and fame are not the same.

604

The aphorist's palliative care: the relief of pain through the careful insertion of innumerable short, sharp needles.

605

If poetry must be understood as a craft and practised as an art, it shouldn't be surprising that occasionally poets understand too much and practise too little.

606

I've heard it said that sex is natural, but surely not. The sex drive may be as natural an instinct as you like. Yet how you accommodate it in your life and in that of another or of others is a matter of cultural opportunities, manners, morals, laws, and customs. Some states of social life offer assistance with that difficult task; others, to put it mildly, will prove a hindrance.

607

The truth has been defined as simply 'a warrantable assertion'. Nonetheless, it's telling—at best times and in right places and in the most judicious words—must be the manifesting of ethical values, and complex ones at that.

608

Keeping going's hard, but keeping believing that you can keep going is something else again.

609

Fear of attack, subliminally or less so, is index-linked to the threat you fear you pose.

610

When the state of technological development means that the use of missiles, air-raids, artillery, cluster bombs, mines, not to mention large and small arms fire, will produce collateral damage (also known as the massacre of the innocent), even so-called just wars will prove the sufficient and necessary causes of war crimes on all sides.

611

Sins of omission and commission: we have been war-ifying crime, when we ought to have been criminalizing war.

612

If writing about things will inevitably appropriate and travesty them, well then, admit it, even the sacred is not sacred.

613

Why, when you can be multi-faceted, why persist in being two-faced?

614

The fragile goodness of artistic products is only too prone to the envious spoiling in disturbed people's critical readings. But, but, but . . . robustly literary verbal structures should be sufficient to show, sooner or later, that the envious spoiling is a backhanded compliment to this very goodness.

615

Spendthrift artists: look how they live beyond their meanings!

616

Given the linguistic bankruptcy of describing a loan as 'sub-prime' when what that means is anything from 'pretty risky' to 'bad', it should surprise no one that financial bankruptcy should inevitably follow at the speed, more or less, of a falling dictionary.

617

There is an odd, and perhaps unsuspected, hubristic smell lingering around the modestly sold human benefits to be reaped in subscribing to the Pragmatist compromise on truth.

618

One difficulty with the pragmatist urging us to believe in fictions, even as we know them to be fictions, for their 'cash value', is that those who need belief in their lives would not count that as the genuine article.

619

Anti-foundationalists invoke their radical skepticism to undermine others' convictions, but hardly ever to hoist that conveniently indiscriminate debunking in its own petard.

620

Buddhists, too, can be stung by insects.

621

The vanity in composing poetry that will resist its own critical recuperation shows in its pretending to the existence of readers motivated enough to wish to recuperate it. Proudly rebarbative styles may only too easily have precluded that too.

622

Politicians and statesmen, if you think the media has been blackening your reputations why not increase your esteem for the independent-mindedness of your electorates?

623

Claiming to be 'wrong about Japan', you'll inevitably be so in a pair of ways: the ones you think you know about, and the ones you don't.

624

A likely explanation for why those indebted to you are not paying you back is that they're awaiting a repayment themselves.

625

No, I'm not trying to change the world, or to live in a better one . . . I'm trying to foster the better and discourage the worse in the no other world than this.

626

No imaginable good can ever come from exploiting the means of your imagined enemies.

627

Tyrannies *can* be constructively killed with kindness, but who among the worldly powers would be willing to give it a try?

628

While it's doubtless true that individuality is stymied in situations where there are no choices, it hardly follows that the more choices available the more individuality you get.

629

Devotion beyond the requirements even of duty only too readily slides into a niggling resentment at seeming to be exploited by the insufficiently grateful.

630

In this world anyone who isn't at least momentarily afraid of going mad cannot be sane.

631

I hear that the North Korean leaders are being invited to give up their nuclear weapons programmes in return for a better future for their people. What a brilliant idea! Could we perhaps do that too?

632

When it comes to human cruelty, our offence is our first and best defence.

633

Writing to the moment: beware, beware, the reality pundits and the Zeitgeist groupies.

634

The journalist who wrote that civilized life could not be sustained without hypocrisy must have something or other in mind for us to hide—but what is there left to reveal?

635

One difficulty with money is that if you don't think about it you'll be robbed, and if you do it will surely corrupt you.

636

More money: if you lose it you'll be ruined, if you don't it ruins you.

637

Economics is the great pseudo-science that rules the world by claiming human values can be expressed as numbers.

638

And when do the powerful not conceal their hand behind the supposed compulsions of accountancy?

639

The reviewer: yet one more endangered species swept way in the tsunami of book publishing.

640

Rembrandt's *Juno*, seen in the Armand Hammer collection alongside a good Fantin-Latour, underlined in the monumentally moving solidity of the ordinary woman, and her vividly living eyes, that the artist's stature was achieved through the transfiguration of his own corporeal clumsiness.

641

A poem is a solid that has an air to the way it flows.

642

The spirit of the stair: 'What did translating poetry teach you?' a student asked me at the end of a reading. 'By requiring that I faithfully recreate the poetry of another, it taught me to respect my own materials.' But that, I'm afraid, is what I thought to reply some time after the class was over.

643

The vast majority of human activity is performed with the implicit assumption that it will lead to nothing but oblivion, and the activity is no less valued or valid for that. Why then should poets be considered heroic because they too work in the face of such nullification? Here, it would seem, is a tacit tribute (if a backhanded one) to poetry's legendary, mythical power of immortalization.

644

You want the moral high ground? Get onto the level playing field then.

645

Ours is a culture fixated on the weighty and the deep. Yet a light touch in an artist need not be any less indelible, and, in its quickness, it might even be more so.

646

You might fairly doubt that—with the right upbringing, education, influences, and experience—the sensibility horizon of human beings is limitless. Yet you would be equally wrong to set definite limits to any one person's horizon of understanding, sensitivity, and compassion.

647

If a thing's self-evident, it's worth explaining.

648

Another fatal misprint: for 'dollarology' read 'dolorology'.

649

Universities, especially their arts and social sciences faculties, are not only, or they're not so much places where new ideas are hatched, as where old ones go to die, painfully slowly sometimes, after they've been unjustly rejected by society—and perhaps, now and then, that's just how time's whirligig brings in its revenges.

650

In self-deception, who is deceiving whom? This smart question doesn't appear to take into account the fact that the self is realized socially, so becoming aware that you may have suffered from a bout of self-deception requires you to be granted a new perspective, and this occurs through social interactions (including reading, of course) over time. In self-deception, an evolving person looks back on a former self-manifestation and feels ashamed. While in the grip of true self-deception, the deceived cannot know they are deceived, and thus the smart question has bite. Nevertheless, it is merely smart, because the 'who' and the 'whom' are readily achieved retrospectively either when someone is criticized (when I think you are wrong about yourself, for example), or through individual retrospection produced by, for instance, realizing the unexpected consequences of falsely confident behaviour.

651

A post-post-modern wager: if I act as if there is a world to which true reference can be made, and understood to have been made, but there isn't such a world, then in effect I'm in the same position as you, who don't, and were right all along. But if it turns out that the burden of evidence and practice tends to support the existence of a reality to which we can successfully refer, then you have fashionably disabled yourself from the very outset. How will we find out? Time alone will tell.

652

Ah all those old communist regimes in which the state was meant to wither away, and did by means of embargoes and frozen assets, though its arthritic bureaucracy remained intact—what will become of our political moralities when none of them are left to salve our tarnished consciences?

653

Eloquently regretting that you'd ever been born, but not so much as to take your own life, is yet another way to take your own existence far too seriously—and, if you are an honest but incorrigible person, to make a song and dance about that too.

654

If, as a friend of mine put it, 'per ardua ad ardua' is the motto of the research-assessed Ivory Tower, 'ars longa vita longa' must be the one for the slum-cleared wastelands of Grub Street and Bohemia.

655

'Gong-tormented': a fellow poet's perfect epithet for the effects of literary prizes and awards on those who attract them, and on those who don't.

656

If the greatest authors are those whose characters are more famous than they are, I award the prize to Mrs. Felicia Hemans for her boy on the burning deck, and offer a very honourable mention to Sir Arthur Conan Doyle for his detective and doctor friend. In this light the great Shakespeare ('where have I heard that name?') far outshines even Hamlet, Ophelia, Romeo, Juliet, Falstaff, and the rest, while Charles Dickens writes in a style designed subliminally to upstage his Pickwick, Oliver, Pip, Estella, Podsnap and all. Hiawatha, or its rhythm, may be about as well known as Longfellow, but I fear that almost all other authors, Jane Austen (notwithstanding Elizabeth and Darcy) included, are much better known than any of the characters they have created.

657

Someone said yesterday that he could face the coming years because he had no imagination; he could take one day at a time. I had to admit it: not only did I have to live a life, I also had to live the fiction of one, and not the former without the later—even if that made everything more difficult, and not only difficult for me.

658

What are you trying to prove? That old question, maybe even a puzzled one, asked by my art teacher back in 1970, keeps coming home to haunt me. Any answer, grammatically speaking, would have to run 'trying to prove that . . .', followed by an assertion supported with demonstrable evidence. But perhaps one difficulty about the question, and not only for a 17-year-old, is that devoting a life to making artworks you'll only discover what it was you were trying to prove after you've done it. This is as true for each individual piece as for an entire oeuvre—and is likely what prompts the defensive riposte that 'really I'm not trying to prove anything at all'.

659

If there's one thing more astonishing than the life of Christ, it's the history of the Church.

660

When it comes to slogans I think I prefer Tower Records' *No music, no life* to Rilke's *Gesang ist Dasein*. After all, the former is the more Shakespearean.

661

You can't translate the sound of a poem in another language—not because you won't be able to approximate the sound of a phrase or line on those rare and lucky occasions where a greater degree of transposition is possible, but because the approximated sound effects are now occurring in an altogether different economy, both macro and micro, of sound-sense relations.

662

It's often difficult to persuade people to imagine life from others' points of view—except when it comes to another's spending power.

663

Though intriguingly asking just how intrinsic it is, Bernard Williams calls trustworthiness an intrinsic value—by which he appears to mean that it is a good in itself. The problem with this definition, he adds, is that it has no descriptive power, while attempted descriptions of why it is a value reductively backslide into instrumentalism. Perhaps the sense that it is an intrinsic value, then, derives from the probability that whatever the human group, from the noblest to the most vicious, trustworthiness is likely to be valued as a good in its perceived contribution to cohesiveness and task efficiency. In this, it is unlike sincerity or unbending truthfulness, which both require highly nuanced situational inflections to be definitively evaluated as goods. Yet if the intrinsic value of trustworthiness comes from its ubiquitous desirability, then, in this case, intrinsic and instrumental are but aspects of the same value.

664

Some philosophers have demonstrated to their satisfaction that just as there is no bebop barrier, so too there is no fact—value distinction. Yet look how the distinction usefully survives in their denial, or even disproof, of its existence.

665

If there's one thing worse than the need of writers to be published, reviewed, and awarded prizes, it's the need some publishers and editors feel to express their will to power by first lording over them, and then, for the unlucky (in Baudelaire's sense), lauding with prizes the supposedly choicest of them.

666

By all means aspire to the stars, but do try not to suck up to them.

667

Review copy, whether laudatory or knocking, so often betrays the note of a patronizing inferiority, or of patronizing inferiority.

668

My children, of Anglo-Italian parentage and living in Japan, spent their first decade or so speaking three languages. The elder, then of kindergarten age, told us that she had invented her own. It was called

Fusco. Naturally, at that age, she was too young to teach it to her parents, even had she wanted. We did, though, learn the name of the language, and we heard some of its phonemes.

669

When a baby cries, reasonable parents run through their repertoire of possible explanations and responses: needs to sleep, needs changing, needs bathing, needs to be held, needs to be fed . . . My own relationship to my sensations and pains feels not unlike that parent-child relationship. I can never be absolutely sure what's causing the complaint, but I hope I'm getting better at running through my minimally extended repertoire.

670

You begin to suffer from a diabetic condition producing, as a consequence, the tendency to lose patience with your close relatives especially around meal times. Later, your medical condition is diagnosed and treated. You then understand that you weren't exactly angry with those around you, but suffering a blood-sugar imbalance. Nevertheless, you *did* quarrel with your family, and not merely *as if* you were irritated at their behaviour. The misrecognition of sensations is not just possible—it's a fairly usual condition of life.

671

Consider the situation of a person, a child perhaps, who receives all sorts of adequate answers to a question without ever losing the irritation, if that's the word, which has prompted the question, or better, the questioning.

672

Yes, I accept that humility is a kind of pride, but I also know which kind I prefer.

673

Yet another literary cliché (*tradutore—traditore*): translators are not usually betrayers because to betray is identified in the intention of an act, not of necessity in a result. The only translators who could be said to betray would be those whose intentions were to travesty. Differences between text and translation are not necessarily signs of betrayal, but merely the terms for a dialogue between verbal products set in a conversational relationship.

674

Recourse to religion when you have shown, at least to your own satisfaction, that all other systems of thought and value will inevitably fail (as in 'The Vanity of Human Wishes' or *Rasselas*) is to take God for a foul weather friend, except that for you it's always raining.

675

If there's one thing more doleful than having your bridges burned before you've crossed them, it's others crossing your bridges for you—before you've even got there.

676

It's by no means easy to alter the habits of a lifetime, especially when you don't have another one to live.

677

Homecoming: it was like turning over stones in a garden to see what there was living still among the yellowed grasses.

UNIVERSITY OF WINCHESTER
LIBRARY

678

There's nothing wrong with feeling homesick, so long as you don't happen to be at home.

679

Successes in life compose a flat picture. Failures make a landscape with shading and recession.

680

Success defeats us. Failures spur us on.

681

It may be, as Emerson says, that to be great is to be misunderstood. Sadly, his words can't help us—for it doesn't follow that being misunderstood we must be great.

682

You can tell by the way people move that they're the ones holding the baby.

683

Pay close attention to what others are doing: their achievements are freeing you to be yourself.

684

When asking 'What is a work of art?' John Carey is driven by the eccentric varieties he can call up to define it as, in effect, anything that anyone has thought of as a work of art and for whatever reason. Aside from the fact that in practice it is by no means anyone who can make such thoughts stick, the tribute this pays to art is that no interested person would accept such a definition of a chess game, say, or a soccer match. The open-ended, democratizing inclusiveness of the definition, however unsatisfactory, underlines a unique relevance for art in life, even as it appears to eclipse it.

685

Phlogiston: Dear God, the fact that we have a word for something hardly guarantees that this something exists!

686

Investing in people sounds like such a good idea. Don't forget, though: the investors are expecting a return for their money.

687

Uncharacteristics: William Hazlitt thinks that 'if a man is disliked by one woman, he will succeed with none'. But if that were true, no divorced man could ever remarry.

688

Glancing in a mirror these days, I'm confronted by a middle-aged stranger who, I realize, is me. Perhaps a day will come when this realization won't occur at all. Momentarily taken for someone else, I'm preparing for that day.

689

Yes, the terracotta warriors of the Chinese emperor massed together in their underground bunkers are coldly terrifying. But how many plebian deaths were required to alleviate, if they so much as could, their emperor's terror of mortality?

690

'Poetry makes nothing happen': as in the quatrain on the stone over Shakespeare's grave, the one cursing 'he that moves my bones'. So far, no one has.

691

You ought to know better than to know best.

692

After these years of changes, I'm nothing if not restless for stability.

693

Because the structures of music are abstract (the pentatonic scale, the twelve-tone row), its elements, however coloured, when combined can be vastly expressive of ideas about life, but they cannot articulate them. In literature, the structures are not abstract but themselves meaning-bearing (the apostrophe, the passive verb phrase, hypotaxis) so their elements, both coloured and meaning-bearing, have to articulate ideas and feelings about life as well as expressing them. Music is the expression of non-articulated propositions, while literature is the articulation of expressive propositions. That's why there can be child prodigies in music, but not in writing.

694

The sex war: after battle was joined men and women became so confused in hand-to-hand fighting that there were no sides left between which to call a truce.

695

Exiled on the far side of the world I approached my home country in imagination and memory; back home, it obliges me to keep a safe distance.

696

God is all seeing, all knowing, and all merciful. He can forgive our sins before we've even got round to committing them.

697

On a problem of forgiveness: it is blasphemous to presume he can and blasphemous to assume he can't; but we, because not divine, always must (although we often can't). Yet how can we be obliged to do what we cannot expect of the divine?

698

A decidedly anti-religious scientist has stolen the unshakeable conviction in what he does from his deadliest enemy.

699

While it makes some sense to say you don't know how the past will turn out, it makes none to ask why we can't remember the future. Present occurrences can change how aspects of the past are perceived, reopen and alter the outcomes of apparently concluded sequences of events—as poets like Shakespeare know. But you would have to be a thorough and strict determinist to think that everything about the future had already occurred, and if it hadn't, then it is only the bad poetry of speculative pseudo-science to suppose that, time reconfigured, it might be remembered 'before' it had happened.

700

Yet more spirit of the stair: not only do writers want to have the late, but not too late, last word, they also want to attach it to the missed occasion by lodging it in the disappeared ear, and in doing so, to hurl it permanently into the future.

701

Yes, the truth sometimes hurts; but falsehood frequently kills.

702

A white lie doesn't have to be a spin-doctored black one.

703

Virtual unreality, yet once more: human civilization used to have a soul; now it barely has a body.

704

'It's the economy, stupid.' 'No, it's the stupid economy.'

705

The only art form in which for century after century the English (and the English-speaking) have produced consistently high achievements is the one they tend to have least time for: poetry.

706

There will be a point in the history of any significant writer's reception when the critics are no longer helping found a reputation and find a readership, but are attracting status to themselves by their association with 'our author'. Yet for those who come after this point the only decent stance will be to act as if unaware that any such status could possibly accrue. All the rest is, more or less, careerism.

707

To the Italian electorate: if you opt for a businessman as your leader, you can't not expect him to make a profit out of his new concern and don't try and kid yourselves that you are his shareholders, because you include the people who didn't vote for him—which is not how limited companies pass on profits.

708

A credit rating: a calculation showing how well you can handle money worked out on the basis of your not having it to handle. Those who have never been in debt, that is, find it difficult to get one.

709

The editor of a dead poet's collected edition notes that 'in drafts you can see her quite often changing words for the improvement of musical effects' and adds that this 'might seem deplorable, if the effects didn't always open out the sense rather than just change it, but it's a rare way to compose.' Rather, it's the only way to compose—if, that is, you understand the music of a poem to be an inseparable part of its sense and purpose.

710

Honest sceptics: people learning to fly by sawing off the branch upon which they are sitting.

711

Consider the sadness of a man who, after a lifetime of continence in matrimony, comes to the mistaken conclusion that he would have been happier deflowering and philandering.

712

You can sometimes hear artists and sports personalities praised by appeals to metempsychosis: so-and-so *is* Eddy Mercx, what's-her-name *is* Edith Piaf . . . Looked at in this light, most of us are the reincarnation of no one in particular.

713

Did Goethe really say 'Habit is a gift from heaven, a substitute for happiness'? Happiness is by definition transitory, and has an opposite— unhappiness—to remind us of the fact. Habit, though, contributes to sustainable stability. Is that what he meant? We can't be always happy, but we can regulate our existences with habit to avoid unhappiness? And what if he had written 'contentment' instead of 'happiness'? That would have made even less sense.

714

The tedium of luxury, like a page by Wallace Stevens . . .

715

The problems with describing English as a national language might begin with the fact that, as UK passport holders are only too aware, there is no English *nation* for which it is the language.

716

A translation is a text that has achieved the distinction of being able to contain mistaken renderings from another language.

717

God knows the things being done in his various names? He must be turning in his grave.

718

Watching a routine bio-pic about the life together and apart of Sylvia Plath and Ted Hughes, I was reminded once again how much it's the very idea of the poet as a flauntedly or reservedly 'different' being which has to be combated by unflagging hard work, self-less dedication, the exercise of irreducibly practical skills, interminable reconsideration, and sensitivity to other people's speech with all its implied thoughts and feelings, betrayed or expressed—in short, by such ordinary qualities as might make some poets (just as they can make anyone) valuably different.

719

After François Villon's 'Mais où sont les neiges d'antan?' and a little poem by Luciano Erba: 'Snow ain't what it used to be. Now it makes the news.'

720

On listening to Bob Dylan read a poem on the radio: the mannered tones of some people's voices must make it all but impossible for them to hear the timbres of literary works. Yet to listen as someone reads a poem out loud in a distinctively accented manner, yet not to hear it as communicating with others, but as echoing inwardly in the speaker's

732

I hear it reported that someone's faith in God has been threatened by the diagnosis of a terminal illness: yet, if so, why had it not been shattered by the daily round of others' apparently unjust deaths? It's as if faith had not been able to teach this person the first thing about its purpose in life.

733

In Chicago, at a reading once, when somebody asked me a question, I was sure I had seen him before, and started as if . . . but I couldn't have done. Yes, this was the day's metaphysical painting: to have been questioned about a translation from Vittorio Sereni by the spitting image of Giorgio de Chirico.

734

Night Watch: a Christmas tree's decked out already on the thirteenth floor. Nobody's in or, wrong, a woman home alone. She sees me in my hotel room, is gone like a Bathsheba holding her mobile. Returned to the glass, now, she closes drapes on snow becoming sleet down North Michigan Avenue. It gusts across a storefront window—one devoted to Rembrandt on his four-hundredth birthday.

735

The Picasso variant of T. S. Eliot's idea that immature poets borrow and mature poets steal, namely that 'good artists copy, great artists steal' has made it onto a T-shirt, I see. But in the fame-crazed anxiety about whether we happen to be immature or great, why not spare a thought for the quality of those that they imitate, those that they borrow from, or from whom they even steal?

736

You want more feedback? But feedback is distortion.

737

The devil is in the cliché!

738

Lying in bed at Southsea during Christmas 1980, I wrote a poem occasioned by a moment the previous summer in which a European Football Championship was associated, by means of the glitter on the waves of Lake Garda, with events from the Second World War and the then current fighting in Afghanistan. The poem's title was the entire section from W. S. Graham's 'Implements in their Places', published in 1977, which reads: 'Feeding the dead is necessary'. Almost thirty years later, I now suspect that Graham had been inspired by a painful episode early in Olivia Manning's *The Danger Tree*, the first volume of *The Levant Trilogy*, also published in 1977. More, the episode in which Sir Desmond and Lady Hooper try to feed their dead son through a hole blown in his face by a grenade is, later in the novel, commented on by Castlebar, a character partly based on Bernard Spencer, in Cairo at the time: 'Egypt's a weird place. Feeding the dead's an ancient custom, but it still goes on.' To have that line of Graham's echo back to the cruelties of distant wars had been closer to the bone than I knew at the time—and was itself being fed by the fictional words of a poet-figure whose original's poems had, even then, been as near to my heart.

739

Why are the 'houses' the shared world and not the 'agreed on perceptions of the houses'? It's because the senses are tools for managing creatures' relations with the world and not, primarily at least, philosophers' tools for finding evidence of its existence. If you are born blind, you will likely hear and smell houses far better than the sighted, and may well employ a trained dog to get you around them. When Doctor Johnson stamped his foot, rebounding off the stone, in an attempt to refute Bishop Berkeley, whatever else he was doing, he was certainly behaving in an odd way—as James Boswell noted.

740

I'm staring at the television and as I look at the weather chart symbols over my hometown I say 'It's raining!' My wife is peering between drawn curtains at the same time and, by chance, simultaneously announces 'It's raining!' We share beliefs. We're equally right. What we don't share are sensory stimuli.

741

A Manifesto for the League of Non-Aligned Poets: because we won't stand for anything, poets of the world, unite! We have nothing to lose . . .

742

Ah life: an aphorism waiting to happen.

Afterword

I hadn't any idea of writing aphorisms, and had thought myself incapable of such mental agilities, until sometime towards the end of the 1990s. The initial impulses came in the form of notebook entries containing thoughts connected with the paradoxes and absurdities associated with the life of poetry and the poet. They were merely isolated jottings, and not made with any thought of publication. It was only during 2002 that, in the lead up to the invasion of Afghanistan and then the Iraq War, I began to formulate and note down thoughts on a variety of topics as they came to mind. This sudden flood of comments and remarks, scribbled down with little thought for their artistic merit, surprised me—and a few of them were formulated to explain to myself what had happened, or was happening, to prompt such an outburst. I had perhaps reached a point in life were the self-censorship of a painfully learned intellectual prudence collapsed under the pressure of the contradictions in my own and the world's evident predicaments.

One such explanation for this form of expression might be that the habit began as a by-product of teaching in a Japanese university. There, because of the students' difficulties with listening comprehension, it had been my practice to formulate the ideas I was attempting to convey, in short and simple sentences that could be copied from the blackboard. Over the years I had come to use this as a means of thinking out loud in a semi-public place. Naturally, these sentences did not tend to include puns or joking paradoxes. Yet the take-off into a form of the same activity, but with the expanded freedom provided by my private notebooks and no thought of publication, might explain how these jottings started to come and then accelerated so unexpectedly.

It's not, of course, that I knew nothing of aphorisms when that began to happen. Brought up in a vicarage, attending Sunday school and church services each week, I had come early into contact with the aphoristically memorable parables and sayings of Jesus Christ. Nor were my parents above laughing at the witticisms of Oscar Wilde in TV broadcasts of *The Importance of Being Earnest*—a play that I was to take parts in every summer for a number of years during the 1980s. Somewhere among my papers there is a translation from Umberto Saba's *Scorciatoie*—made simply to understand what it was saying in about 1991 or 1992, and I was asked to translate a few more by him and Maria Luisa Spaziani for *Geary's Guide to the World's Great*

UNIVERSITY OF WINCHESTER LIBRARY

Aphorists (Bloomsbury, 2007). While a graduate student I read some of Wittgenstein's philosophical writings and, later, through comments on his work, also Karl Kraus, then the more aphoristic Nietzsche, then Lichtenberg and others. More promptings came from the *Unquiet Grave* by Cyril Connolly and Geoffrey Grigson's remarks on the life of writing in *The Private Art*.

Perhaps a final element to add into this mix of sources would be the influence of two kinds of poetry: the first is the short prose poem, as developed by Pierre Reverdy out of Rimbaud and Baudelaire, and the second is the Japanese short poem—the tanka and haiku. Gathered here, then, is a series of hybrid writings that I first brought together, set down, or sequenced at intervals over some years before, as I say, the possibility of publication arose. Three hundred and fifty-four pieces appeared under the name *Untitled Deeds* in a 2004 collection that also included other short prose pieces. In the present collection, that set of aphorisms is reprinted entire. Those from number 355 to the end are selected from a collection whose working title was *Further Trespasses*, adopted to indicate that these aphorisms are a continuation of that earlier work, that I've been straying into territory not my own yet once more, and to attempt a slight bow in the direction of the Greek etymology of the word 'aphorism', from 'boundary' or 'limit'. Perhaps one way to read them is to go as far as their limits will allow, then use them as prompts to think beyond those boundaries. The umbrella title of this selection, adapted from the well-known French expression, *l'esprit d'escalier*, tells its own story.

Certainly one of the things that will have started these words was the element of risk in articulating thoughts and feelings just as they came to mind and in so naked a form. Kraus's title, *Half Truths and One-and-a Half Truths*, invites us to remember that aphorisms often work by angled partiality and pertinent exaggeration. Whether the following pieces even rise to such levels of truth is for others to say. I can only hope they occasion for readers something of the assistance, diversion, and relief that writing them has given me.

Peter Robinson
30 September 2008

Acknowledgements

Aphorisms from the first part of this selection were originally published in *Untitled Deeds* (Salt Publications, 2004). My thanks go to Chris and Jen Hamilton-Emery both for their work on that book and for permission to reprint them here. Some of the aphorisms from the second part appeared in John Tranter's Internet magazine *Jacket* no. 28 (October 2005), and in James Geary, *Geary's Guide to the World's Great Aphorists* (Bloomsbury, 2007), while John Matthias chose a selection entitled 'Practical Utopianism' for the *Notre Dame Review* no. 29 (autumn 2009). I would like to thank these writers for their support and encouragement.

UNIVERSITY OF WINCHESTER
LIBRARY

Lightning Source UK Ltd.
Milton Keynes UK
04 October 2009

144534UK00001BA/241/P

9 781848 610620